ISD
From the Ground Up

A No-Nonsense Approach
to Instructional Design

Chuck Hodell

ASTD
PRESS

Alexandria, Virginia

ASTD Press is an internationally renowned source of insightful and practical information on workplace learning and performance topics, including training basics, evaluation and return on investment, instructional systems development, e-learning, leadership, and career development.

Ordering information: Books published by ASTD Press can be purchased by visiting ASTD's website at store.astd.org or by calling 800.628.2783 or 703.683.8100.

Library of Congress Control Number: 2010925221

ISBN-10: 1-56286-743-1
ISBN-13: 978-1-56286-743-0

ASTD Press Editorial Staff:

Director: Anthony Allen
Manager, ASTD Press: Larry Fox
Project Manager, Content Acquisition: Justin Brusino
Senior Associate Editor: Tora Estep
Associate Editor: Ashley McDonald
Editorial Assistant: Stephanie Castellano

Copyeditors: Abella Publishing Services
Indexer: Abella Publishing Services
Proofreader: Abella Publishing Services
Interior Design and Production: Kathleen Schaner
Cover Design: Steve Fife

Printed by Sheridan Books, Inc., Chelsea, MI 48118

◆ Contents

◆ Preface

"Up"—as we have come to call this book over its several editions and more than ten years in print—has its roots in trying to find a way to simply and effectively teach the basics of instructional systems development (ISD) to new students of the process while also serving as a reference for experienced practitioners.

From the very beginning of my work on this effort, my ISD mentor, Dr. J. Marvin Cook, urged me not to make this strictly a scholarly work, but to make it a practical guide that would offer something for everyone who was interested in instructional design. With his influence and my writer's mantra of "make sure they can use this every day," I have endeavored to make this a clear and concise guide to ISD to serve both new and experienced instructional designers.

If a reader takes anything from this book, I hope it is the idea that instructional design is a system dynamic enough to work with any set of variables regardless of the particulars. Any learning environment from social media to classroom lectures can be a powerful and successful learning experience, and ISD allows designers the opportunity to pull it all together using a systems approach to instructional design.

Why a Third Edition?

Since the second edition of this book was published in 2006, many readers have asked that I include even more instructional design tools for the more advanced designers. These needs were most often expressed by educators involved in programs that use this book as a text either in undergraduate or master's-level education programs and courses. This third edition includes new and exclusive chapters introducing the content mastery continuum and the mastery tipping point as well as new chapters on social media, ISD history, and the practice of giving back to the community by performing work pro bono.

Acknowledgments

Without ISD pioneer Dr. J. Marvin Cook, this book and my practice of ISD would never have happened. His patient and loving mantra of "make everyone a winner" still resonates in his students and all who know him. I also wish to express appreciation to the folks at ASTD for their partnership with me on this effort; to Dr. Greg Williams, my partner at the graduate program in ISD at UMBC; to my colleagues at UMBC, including Sharese Essien, Debra Petska, Zane Berge, Jeannette Campos, Paul Kellerman, Keith Curran, Carol Erdman, Todd Marks, Greg Walsh, and Linda Raudenbush; to all of my students through my many years as a teacher; and finally to my friend and partner Karen Smith, for keeping me "real" through all of this.

Dedication

To the loves of my life, my children Heather, David, and Joe. All I do in life is a reflection of my commitment to you as your dad.

Chuck Hodell
Kent Island, Maryland, 2011

Introduction

Handbook for Instructional Designers

The practice of instructional design as a profession is now more than 50 years old. From its early beginnings as a process without a name to the more recent global recognition of the value of instructional design as an able partner in education and training for commercial and nonprofit organizations, ISD (instructional systems development) has matured step-by-step, or more recently technology-by-technology, as the world has quickly grown from one-room schoolhouses to one learner in front of a laptop.

As the field of instructional design has grown, so has the need for competent and talented instructional designers. In every corner of the world, instructional designers are assisting in building ever more complex learning networks linking content with eager learners of every age.

One benefit from all of this recognition for ISD is that many non-ISD professionals now realize that a percentage of what they do every day is teach or train others. The practice of instructional systems development is often such a transparent enterprise that many practitioners fail to recognize their role as an instructional designer. They think of themselves as managers, supervisors, human resources professionals, nurses, lawyers, physicians, and thousands of other occupations that don't fall neatly into the education and training environment. They don't realize that they have many of the same instructional design challenges that confront teachers, facilitators, trainers, and academics every day.

Every instructional designer has started in the same place in this field—at the beginning. Some learn experientially through trial and error, often consulting a book or website for ideas, whereas others have the advantage of being mentored

> The truth is that countless instructional designers exist in every location where a teacher stands in front of a classroom, an apprenticeship instructor teaches a skilled trade, a trainer gathers a group in the company conference room for an orientation session, a supervisor mentors a new employee, a nurse shows patients how to care for themselves, or a volunteer works with an underserved population in a small unlit meeting room in a village or hamlet in some corner of the world. Instructional designers are everywhere, and they are seldom recognized for their contributions or given any tangible support in their efforts.
>
> This is one reason *ISD From the Ground Up* was originally written and, now in its third edition, strives to provide every designer a handbook of skills to refer to or learn as it fits his or her needs and level of experience.

by a veteran designer. This book offers the benefits of a handbook and a mentor and makes them each readily available, perhaps next to your computer or in your briefcase.

This book provides both novice and experienced instructional designers a series of tools to reference as they practice their profession. Included are such basics as the ADDIE (analysis, design, development, implementation, and evaluation) model of ISD, analysis tools, tips on how to write objectives, and the two essential deliverables in ISD—the design plan and the lesson plan.

For designers seeking more advanced tools, this edition includes several new chapters that include the introduction of the content mastery continuum and mastery tipping point as well as new chapters about social networking and using learning management systems. If you have ever worked with subject matter experts, you will undoubtedly appreciate the new chapter on working with them. Additional new chapters help you develop your own personal ISD portfolio and invite you to consider pro bono work as a way to give back to your community. And finally, for the first time, an exhaustive glossary of ISD terms is included.

Designer's Handbook

This book is designed to be a designer's handbook as well as a text for students taking graduate or undergraduate instructional design courses. As such, the focus is on practical knowledge and everyday issues that a professional instructional designer is likely to face.

Almost every topic in this book could support an entire book in its own right, and no attempt is made to cover every theoretical or operational variant on a topic. What is represented is a guide to the challenges most likely to be encountered by an instructional designer working in the field. ASTD has an entire library of excellent publications on many of the topics mentioned in this text, and I encourage you to review everything that is available to you from all available sources.

This book gives you the chance to practice ISD skills as you read, and discussion questions are designed for both individual review and for group discussion either in the classroom or online in a discussion board or blog.

Pay special attention to the chapters that cover topics of interest to you and to any challenges or questions that arise as your career advances. The essential ISD skills you will learn or review include the following:

- analyzing systems, both general and instructional
- defining and working with the generic ADDIE model of instructional design, performing various analysis operations including population and task analysis, and designing and implementing focus group sessions
- writing objectives and evaluation tasks, and performing other design-phase tasks
- constructing design plans and lesson plans
- performing skills related to the development phase including pilot testing and materials development
- implementing designers' tools
- writing and implementing various evaluation strategies, including Kirkpatrick's four levels of evaluation
- using skills related to social networking and web-based training.

The advanced skills you will have at your fingertips include:

- content mastery continuum (CMC)
- mastery tipping point (MTP)
- quality rating for objectives (QRO)
- quality rating for design plans (QRDP)
- quality rating for lesson plans (QRLP)
- the criticality matrix
- designing for credit.

Instructional design isn't any more difficult to learn and put to use than any other professional process; however, a gap exists between the great and the marginal designs in the real world. There are as many different ways to design a new-employee orientation as there are new employees, but few actually make a new employee feel as if he or she made the right decision in picking a new employer. The difference between a great orientation and a marginal orientation is often in the use of ISD to design training. The use of a system to design and implement the program pays dividends in the way training "feels" to the participants and the benefits it offers an organization.

Instructional systems development (ISD) is a systems approach to training. You may hear it called instructional development, instructional systems design, systems approach to training, or several other terms. They all refer to similar approaches to designing curriculum. You will find while working your way through this book that ISD is really often nothing more than common sense with a plan. Sometimes it just takes someone to point out the relationship between different aspects of instructional design and offer methodologies and shortcuts to make the process more efficient. What commonly defines a professional is the ability to make something look easy. After learning and practicing the basics of ISD you will be moving toward becoming a professional instructional designer.

Though it may look easy to the uninitiated, ISD is a complex set of skills that must be mastered. From the outside, it appears that designing a curriculum is a straightforward process, but below the surface a number of design skills and processes combine to form a project of mythic proportions. New-employee orientation becomes the organizational equivalent to the pyramids—something that stands the test of time.

What Skills Are Required?

A number of specialized skills must be present in an instructional designer's tool kit. The designer's tool kit consists of a variety of both basic and advanced instructional design tools for use one at a time or in combination to form a battery of skills to address one or a hundred design challenges.

Read through the list of instructional design skills in table 1.1, and determine if you have each skill. This is not a test. It only serves as a snapshot of where you begin the process of building your tool kit. For right now, check "yes" or "no" to the questions posed in the table. Later, you will have an opportunity to compare your beginning skills with your ending skills.

Building Your Design Skills

You have the luxury of using this book several ways, depending on your needs. Whether working on a design project or brushing up on a specific aspect of instructional design, you can consult the chapters that fit your needs. If you are just starting out in the field and are not working on a specific project, you can get an in-depth look at the steps of an instructional design project.

Table 1.1. Skills Inventory

Do You Know How to...	Yes	No
Conduct a population analysis?	☐	☐
Design and implement a focus group session?	☐	☐
Write four-part objectives?	☐	☐
Name the four objective domains?	☐	☐
Define and provide examples of at least three instructional methods?	☐	☐
Define and provide examples of at least three distribution methods?	☐	☐
Write at least two evaluation tasks?	☐	☐
Explain the performance agreement principle using an example?	☐	☐
Design evaluations for each of the four Kirkpatrick levels?	☐	☐
Complete a design plan?	☐	☐
Construct a lesson plan?	☐	☐

The book follows one instructional design project—construction of a poison prevention course—from start to finish so you can see how it is done. The subject matter is not intended for actual implementation but to illustrate the instructional design process. After reading each description of the poison prevention project, you may return to it, substituting a project you are working on or any other subject matter you choose. The poison prevention material is intended to serve as a place-holder for your own content.

Who Needs This Book?

This book is a practitioner's guide to ISD and is grounded more in reality than scores of other textbooks are. Novice designers will find this book a useful and practical guide, without a great deal of academic theory. Advanced practitioners will find it an excellent in-service resource for reviewing their skills and then adding new skills to an already impressive resume of ISD knowledge and practice.

Both new and seasoned practitioners will find that this book provides the basics of great instructional practice as well as practical ways to apply the principles. The book is useful for designers at any level of experience or working in any design environment, including small or large organizations, nonprofits or corporations, and schools or training centers. One of the biggest myths about instructional design is that it is really only useful when integrated in a large organization. Nothing could be further from the truth. In fact, the largest gains in efficiency and participant success are often in environments that are either strapped for resources, such as nonprofits and community groups, or in one-person operations, such as classroom teachers or small training organizations. This is true for several reasons, not the least of which is that even incremental moves toward efficiency in small organizations reap great advantages.

Another advantage of this book is that it allows a designer to review previous work and gauge where projects might be improved or updated. No course is ever more than 90 percent complete if you work from the premise that every project can be improved. Review is an essential part of all instructional design, no matter how well done, even a design that is completed using this book as a guide. As with any creative process, time may change one's perspective. The design that seemed perfect two days before may suddenly appear seriously flawed. This is one advantage of a systems approach to instructional design, given that evaluation is essential to the design process. Even a short period of time will yield improvements when evaluation is conducted with an objective eye. It is the ISD equivalent of counting to 10 when someone's upset and wants to speak his or her mind. Evaluation provides time for reflection and reconsideration.

Accumulation of Advantages

If you play chess, you have probably heard the term *accumulation of advantages*. To a chess master, it means that a player has to complete a number of individual steps correctly in order to win a match. Most great chess players are thinking many moves ahead in order to chart out a strategy and prepare a defense to counter any move an opponent might make.

In ISD, accumulation of advantages is about making sure a designer makes all the right moves when designing curriculum. For example, it is impossible to have a great project if a designer leaves out analysis or evaluation. A designer needs to be three steps ahead of any problems in implementing a project and providing solutions when they do arise. For the chess player or the instructional designer, accumulation of advantages is a concept that means winning, and a designer always wants a winning project.

How This Book Is Arranged

This book is presented with a practitioner's eye toward instructional design, not as an academic look at the subject. Although there are many excellent publications that cover theoretical issues associated with ISD, rank-and-file instructional designers generally appreciate a just-in-time approach to ISD that includes readily implementable tools and processes.

This book contains seven sections designed to help you build or enhance your skills as an instructional designer. This is what you will find in each section:

- ◆ Section I, "The Basics of ISD," contains the essentials of ISD. It sets the foundation for the remainder of your travels through the book as you visit systems and learn why an instructional system is integral to success as an instructional designer. The poison prevention project begins here.

- ◆ Section II, "ADDIE Elements," is the nucleus of ISD as you explore analysis, design, development, implementation, and evaluation in greater detail.

- ◆ Section III, "Objectives," provides incredible practical detail on every aspect of objectives with the inclusion of both how to write them and how they are divided into various domains.

- ◆ Section IV, "Design and Lesson Plans," provides you with both a design plan and a lesson plan, which serve as both learning tools and job aids. You can use these tools to assemble your own projects or just use the model as a point of reference. The poison prevention project takes final form here.

- ◆ Section V, "Quality Control," allows the more advanced instructional designer a chance to review state-of-the-art quality review processes in three key ISD areas: objectives, design plans, and lesson plans.

- ◆ Section VI, "Advanced ISD Topics," takes you into the new areas of the content mastery continuum and the mastery tipping point. This section provides a step-by-step guide to conducting focus groups as well as the new design challenges involved in social networking. You will also find strategies for making tough content decisions using a criticality matrix. Finally, the notion of designing a course with the option of seeking college creditworthiness for the course is discussed.

- ◆ Section VII, "Tips for Success," covers skills enhancement and looks to the future. It also invites you to give back with pro bono design offerings.

The chapters in each section relate to specific themes in instructional design. The arrangement of each topic allows you to quickly analyze your needs in a specific design area and move to where you need to be.

The book concludes with a list of additional resources to guide those who want to know more about ISD, including practical applications and theory. A glossary of

ISD terms is a much-requested addition to this edition of *ISD From the Ground Up* and is an exhaustive guide to the new instructional designer.

Make the most of this book by taking the time to read and apply what you learn as quickly as possible. The accumulation of advantages concept really does work in instructional design.

Read, learn, and apply. And pass it on.

◆ Section I

The Basics of ISD

Chapter 1

A Brief Unofficial History of ISD

Chapter Objectives

At the conclusion of this chapter, you should be able to

- ◆ describe a brief history of ISD
- ◆ name at least three individuals important to the history of ISD.

As you probably already know if you have ever looked for one, formal histories of ISD are usually relegated to a page or two on the occasional website. Instructional design is a professional endeavor that doesn't rely on a rich history or linkage with anyone particularly famous outside of academia to bolster its image or to feed its success. In fact, it seems to delight in its somewhat obscure origins.

While this anonymity isn't a negative, spending a little time looking at how ISD evolved certainly adds a foundation of confidence to new designers and a historical background to the more experienced. There are some very important personalities and moments in the development of the ISD as we know it today that are worth reviewing. And a brief look back reveals that ISD has a rich professional heritage and direct connections to its building blocks of education, psychology, and systems.

To capture a real sense of the history of instructional design, it is necessary to suspend for a moment the notion that ISD is a recent discovery or that there was at any point a beginning that can be dated or confirmed. One person learning from another has no meaningful historical beginning, and even knowing the date would add nothing to the practice of ISD. Teaching and learning are ingrained behaviors, and instructional design at its core is simply a more efficient way to pass knowledge.

That being said, accurate historical reference is possible given our knowledge of the personalities and documentation that have built the foundation of ISD as we know it today. Robert Gagne, Robert Mager, B.F. Skinner, Robert Glaser, Benjamin Bloom, Dr. J. Marvin Cook, and hundreds of others provided the foundation for the practice of instructional design. What has changed exponentially over the last 70 years is the manner in which ISD has matured and gained visibility.

Let's look at several key elements of ISD and how they relate to form the system we identify today as instructional systems development.

Systems Theory

At the base of the modern instructional systems approach to curriculum development is the foundational work on systems theory by Ludwig von Bertalanffy in the 1940s. Systems theory teaches us that the whole is always greater than the sum of the parts. In ISD terms this means that using a system to develop education and training programs provides the best opportunity to bring learners to mastery.

Systems are everywhere in our world and are more sure than the famous death-and-taxes absolutes often wistfully associated with daily life. In fact, systems include death and taxes and everything else in our lives. There is a system associated with every facet of our world, and the more we are in resonance with that logic, the more we are able to function efficiently and effectively. The recognition that training and education are both systems leads us directly to the logical notion that curriculum development is more productive when utilizing a systems approach like ISD. In fact, systems is its middle name.

Educational Mentors and Milestones

Once the systems foundation was in place, it was time for the great minds in education and psychology to define the system elements within the instructional design process. The theoretical and conceptual underpinnings of modern ISD are supported by the work of five ISD mentors: B.F. Skinner, Benjamin Bloom, Robert Mager, Robert Glaser, and Robert Gagne. The early practice of ISD didn't yet have a name but it certainly had direction, and that direction was toward a process that allowed for efficient and replicable instruction and training.

B.F. Skinner

Best known as the father of behaviorism, Skinner was responsible for much of the early thinking in the area of operant behavior and his creation of the operant conditioning chamber, more commonly known as the Skinner box. His influence in Gagne's nine events can be seen in his thoughts on sequencing of learning events and the need for reinforcement and feedback in the learning process.

Skinner later devised a teaching machine that provided practice and feedback much in the same way a tutor reviews content with a student and provides necessary content correction as necessary. The teaching machine didn't actually teach anything new, it was the process of providing learners practice and feedback that later influenced the way lesson plans are designed in the practice of ISD today.

Benjamin Bloom

Bloom's taxonomy is a mainstay in modern education and training and relates to the six levels of complexity in cognitive thought. There are different versions of these taxonomies for three of the objective domains you will study later in chapter 9 namely: cognitive, affective, and psychomotor.

The latest version of Bloom's taxonomy has six levels and is hierarchical in nature. The levels, from entry to exit, are remembering, understanding, applying, analyzing, evaluating, and creating. These directly relate to the content mastery continuum that you will study later in this book in chapter 15.

Bloom's major contribution to ISD is his classifications of hierarchal learning stages that reflect learner progress on a continuum from novice to expert or, if you prefer, entry to exit. This acknowledgement of the importance of sequencing content in instructional design is a key building block of ISD as practiced today. Without recognition of a learner's hierarchical journey to mastery, there is no design process for the staging of content in even the most basic content areas.

Robert Mager

The concepts related to behavioral objectives is considered by most ISD practitioners as the one irreplaceable element of instructional design. You would be hard pressed to find any professionally designed education or training course without them, and we have Robert Mager to thank for that.

Mager wrote that behavioral objectives should have three parts:

1. Behavior
2. Condition
3. Standard

This is very similar to the objectives basics of audience, behavior, condition, and degree we learn in this book in chapter 9.

Mager's 1962 work, *Preparing Instructional Objectives,* set the groundwork for criterion-referenced approaches to objectives and evaluation. ISD may never have matured the way it has without Mager's contributions.

Robert Glaser

While early systems theory was advanced by von Bertalanffy in the 1940s, by the 1960s systems theory had evolved to a more operational level in education and training as Robert Glaser began writing about instructional systems. His system of instruction, as introduced in his 1962 work, *Psychology and Instructional Technology,* consisted of:

1. Instructional goals
2. Entering behavior
3. Instructional procedures
4. Performance assessment

Today, the ADDIE model of ISD, as you will learn in this book, consists of the elements of analysis, design, development, implementation, and evaluation.

Glaser coined the term *terminal* when referring to the final or end mastery for a learner. Today we speak of terminal and enabling objectives; between Mager and Glaser we have the foundation for both systems and objectives. Glaser was responsible for advancing the discussion of what he perceived as the differences between training and learning.

Robert Gagne

Although most commonly remembered for his "nine events of instruction," Robert Gagne also had a profound influence on the early foundational work on the formation of ISD as a process. His work with Leslie Briggs brought forth the concept, and later the practice, of breaking courses into discrete learning events and building instruction after thoroughly analyzing each element. This systems approach to instructional design evolved into the formalized ISD process used today.

Gagne's nine events of instruction are still the basis of most lesson plans and find success in any type of learning delivery system from online and distance learning to more traditional classrooms or blended courses. We will spend much more time later with the nine events in chapter 11.

Dr. J. Marvin Cook

One of the milestones that ushered in the acceptance and professional standing of ISD was the creation of academic courses and programs associated with the theory and practice of instructional design. Throughout the country, degree programs began to emerge at Florida State, Ohio State, Indiana, Syracuse, and other outstanding universities.

In 1968, the newly opened University of Maryland Baltimore County approved its first graduate program, and it was Instructional Systems Development, under the leadership of Dr. J. Marvin Cook. This important milestone provided ISD with both graduate-level standing and an academic visibility that allowed the process to grow and flourish in a supportive academic environment.

Dr. Cook's work within the K–12, military, and corporate environments stands as a testament to ISD's utility and the fact that instructional design is not dependent on a particular population, implementation modality, or learning environment. Thousands of designers now hold advanced degrees and graduate-level certificates thanks to the efforts of Dr. Cook and the other early academic supporters of ISD.

Where It All Leads from Here

With the advent of online learning and the more traditional distance learning coming into a new era of acceptance, ISD has never been more necessary or appreciated. While we honor how instructional design gained acceptance and flourished, a new generation of designers and learning professionals will take ISD to the next level—one we haven't even imagined yet. And that is the strength of this process. No matter what the challenge, going back to the basics of ISD will lead designers to solutions regardless of the population, technology, or delivery system.

In Conclusion

Having a sense of the important milestones and personalities in ISD provides a strong foundation in support of the practice of instructional design. Since ISD is most often associated with process, not personalities, having some knowledge of its past adds a further dimension.

Discussion Questions

1. Do you think ISD is an art or a science or both?
2. Is there a relationship between ISD and the field of psychology?
3. Is academic standing important to instructional designers?

Chapter 2

ISD Practices
and Principles

Chapter Objectives

At the conclusion of this chapter, you should be able to

◆ discuss at least two of the ISD practices and principles mentioned in this chapter.

As our brief history of ISD has shown, instructional systems development has been in existence for a long time. Even though ISD is now recognized and implemented worldwide, there are many facets of the ISD process that are misunderstood or underappreciated. ISD in its purist form is simply a system for the design, implementation, and evaluation of instruction.

ISD Is Timeless

One of the most valuable assets of ISD is that the process of instructional design doesn't change based on decisions made on any individual design issue. Whether a designer chooses online, in class, asynchronous, or distributed implementation methodology doesn't in any way impact ISD as a process. These decisions are based on a number of design elements that are explored in the analysis phase of the ISD process.

The timelessness of ISD means several important things to a designer and to organizations. First, no matter when a designer learns and practices the ISD process, the process doesn't change. It also means that whatever new technologies make their way into the instructional landscape, they can be easily incorporated into an instructional program. The term *keeping current* as used in ISD simply means keeping up with the trends in various aspects of analysis, development, implementation, and evaluation—not the ISD process used to make these necessary design decisions.

ISD Has No Opinions

The neutrality of the ISD process is vital to its effectiveness as a system. It doesn't contain any inherent bias or preconceived notions about any aspect of a particular design process.

With ISD there is no preordained way to solve a specific design issue. Every decision evolves from gathering data and making the best choices available. The system guides the process and the variables inform decisions.

ISD Doesn't Have a Bias Toward a Specific Delivery System

It seems that every new technology or learning model spawns a new approach to implementing instruction, and these are almost always systemically no different than the last big thing in education and training. Multimedia, distance learning, social networking, and tablet computing all have a place in effective instructional programs; however, the process of designing curriculum is not influenced by any of these technologies. ISD guides a design decision; it never makes one, although the choices are usually pretty obvious after analysis is completed.

ISD Identifies Design Problems

One very basic axiom of the ISD process is, "If you are having a problem with a specific ISD design task, it is probably because there is something wrong with the design." More simply put, design problems are usually at fault when the design process stalls. Suppose a designer is struggling with writing a lesson plan and making the content work with the population. The problem is not usually the designer's lack of skill. More often, it is that the population is probably not well defined or is too diverse for the design approach.

For example, including five-year-olds in the same class as adults in content areas like art or music appreciation is almost impossible due to the obvious differences in learning styles, attention spans, and motivation. If the objectives are not related to building a bond between the populations, then separate them into two courses and design for each population separately.

Another example is when a designer can't write behavioral objectives for a very simple content area. Closer examination reveals that the course is actually a conference seminar where participants simply attend and do not in any practical way participate. A designer can never write behavioral objectives for this type of event because there is seldom real learning taking place, and students can't be evaluated. The choice then becomes either to admit that this session is not training and forgo designing a course around it or to upgrade the course to something real that offers lasting instructional value.

In Conclusion

The practice of ISD is built upon several very simple, yet fundamental truths. It has no point of view or bias toward any specific design solutions. It is simply a system that provides a reasoned and tested approach to developing training and education solutions regardless of the individual variables within a specific design scenario.

Discussion Questions

1. How does the timelessness of ISD affect the incorporation of new technologies into an instructional program?
2. What is it about the ISD process that allows it to make design problems self-evident?

Instructional Systems Development and the ADDIE Model

Chapter Objectives

At the conclusion of this chapter, you should be able to

◆ define the term *instructional systems development (ISD)*

◆ define the ADDIE model of ISD

◆ list advantages and disadvantages of instructional systems.

Instructional Systems Development

The term *instructional systems development*, or ISD as it is commonly called, is the general label for a variety of curriculum development elements. Within the framework of ISD resides an entire universe of people, processes, and products that supports learning. In its most generic form, ISD applies to any educational or training environment. Early childhood learning activities for toddlers are just as at home with ISD as corporate training or higher education endeavors. Classroom courses and online learning share a common genesis and process. Learning theories ranging from behaviorist to constructivist have a home in ISD. These are the real strengths of the ISD process. The framework created by this system provides a path to success for every conceivable variable of population, content, and delivery system. To borrow from Socrates, ISD is the journey, not the destination.

Irreplaceable and central in ISD is the instructional designer. Sometimes designers are called curriculum specialists or instructional technicians, but regardless of the nomenclature used, a designer is the touchstone for everything that happens in course development. Designers are part project manager and part facilitator. They often juggle team building with crisis intervention. Without designers you have chaos, and any attempt at implementing systems thinking into curriculum development is difficult if not impossible.

One false assumption that is often nested in the thoughts of novice designers and training managers is that instructional designers have to be subject matter experts (SMEs) in any course they are designing. Some mistakenly believe that design skills have to be joined with specific mastery of a content area for ISD to work. On the surface this seems logical and therefore easy to accept. Digging deeper we find that course content is only one variable in a group of variables that are involved in ISD. Working with SMEs is a designer's skill that negates any requirement for content mastery in a designer. In fact, there are even times when a designer can have too much knowledge of the subject matter and miss fundamental elements of a skill or concept because it is too basic or ingrained to the designer.

A Collective Approach

The notion of starting with nothing and finishing with something of value has a great deal of appeal to most of us. Turning a pile of lumber into a house or 10 yards of fabric into curtains demonstrates creativity and manifests a sense of accomplishment. But these efforts don't start in a vacuum. You cannot build a house or sew curtains unless you start with the right raw materials and have enough correct information to successfully complete the project.

Isaac Newton has long been quoted as saying that his incredible accomplishments in physics were just the result of his "standing on the shoulders of giants." The wisdom and modesty reflected in that statement aside, what Newton was alluding to was the cumulative effect of individual efforts gathered together. Instructional designers do well to identify with the simple truth of this concept: Work with all the best people, gather all the right data, determine how they best fit together, and then design something more significant than each of the single elements alone.

Systems Theory and Curriculum Development

Systems are very simple in concept and often extremely complex in practice. ISD is no different. Most systems contain three basic elements (input, process, and output), and the application of these three elements is the heart of our instructional system. From the perspective of an instructional designer, any undertaking that includes a learner and the subject matter necessary to learn requires an instructional system. Instructional designers need inputs (subject matter and resources), a process (ISD), and outputs (curriculum and materials) to build a training course. This combination of elements is our instructional system.

The term *systems analysis* has been used in countless contexts to reflect the process of analyzing the various elements of a system and determining the interaction of each system element to other same-system elements and interaction of all related individual systems to each other. System analysis can prove to be a very intricate undertaking depending on the complexity of each system and its elements. In ISD, the focus is on the elements and systems that influence course design and development, specifically from the perspective of the designer and the requirements for a sound instructional design process and product.

Like any system analysis, in ISD the instructional designer is looking for ways to make better decisions and thereby create better course and program designs than would have resulted without taking the design process to this level of sophistication. Thorough analysis of all the elements in a specific training or educational system provides a designer the foundation for the traditional design process of producing course materials, lesson plans, and so forth. It is the very heart of the design plan process.

System-speak also includes terms like *policy analysis, cost-benefit analysis, feasibility analysis,* and *consequence analysis.* These are all subsets of the process and are important to review if you are going to become firmly rooted in the systems process. For this book, the focus is on the ISD model known as ADDIE.

Key Systems Definitions
- An *instructional system* is an organized and arranged collection of instructional resources that, when combined, achieve the goal of addressing and providing appropriate training solutions.
- An *extended instructional system* comprises all elements external to the instructional system that have the potential to affect the design process.
- A *project* is a single design effort using an instructional system's approach. The three forms of projects are as follows:
  — *singular:* one designer working alone to complete a project
  — *multiple:* more than one designer usually operating within a single departmental or organizational unit
  — *matrixed:* a combination of designers working with other organizational units.

ADDIE Model

Most designers utilize an instructional system that has five elements: analysis, design, development, implementation, and evaluation. This model is commonly referred to as the ADDIE model, after the first letter of each word. ADDIE is used around the world and all other ISD models or approaches use these five elements even though they may be called something else.

The ADDIE model or some derivative of it provides designers with the necessary structure for designing any curriculum, regardless of the variables involved. Anything from classroom lecture to distance learning starts and ends with the same fundamentals—the ADDIE model.

In the ADDIE model, analysis is the input element for the system; design, development, and evaluation are the process elements; and implementation is the output element. These elements overlap somewhat, depending on the project, and because the system is dynamic, there will be some sharing of duties. This book examines in depth each of the five elements of the ADDIE model, which are briefly described in the following sections.

Analysis

Analysis is the data-gathering element of instructional design. Here, instructional designers assemble all the information they can possibly gather about the project before they consider anything else. Decisions about every aspect of the project must eventually be made. The information that instructional designers gather at this stage will be put to use throughout the system, so it is necessary that they have every scrap of data to ensure the design will be successful.

Design

Design is the blueprinting stage of instructional systems during which instructional designers create the blueprint for a project with all the specifications necessary to complete the project. During this stage, instructional designers write the objectives, construct course content, and complete the design plan.

Development

Materials production and pilot testing are the hallmarks of development. At this stage, most non-designers begin to see progress. Everything from lecture notes to virtual reality is brought from design to deliverable.

Before instructional designers move from development to implementation, it is wise for them to do pilot testing to ensure that deliverables do not have to be redeveloped. Because of the time and expense involved, no one wants to reprint manuals or recode a technology-based project after it goes into implementation. The pilot testing process allows organizations to implement any necessary changes in the project before the expenses associated with materials development are realized. The time and effort expended in pilot testing is well worth the effort for this reason alone. Pilot testing also helps designers feel confident that what they have designed works.

Implementation

The most familiar of the elements is implementation. At implementation, the design plan meets the learner and the content is delivered. The evaluation process that most designers and learners are familiar with takes place in this element. Evaluation is used to gauge the degree to which learners meet objectives and facilitators or technologies deliver the project.

Evaluation

Evaluation doesn't deserve to be listed last in the ADDIE model because it takes place in every element and surrounds the instructional design process. Evaluation is a constant guard at the gate of failure.

The advantages of using an instructional system are numerous, the most important being the ability to design projects quickly and efficiently. Nothing is left to chance or ignored when a designer stays within the framework of the ADDIE or other ISD models. One possible disadvantage is the necessity of a designer to be familiar with the ISD process.

The ADDIE Model at Work

To frame the ADDIE model in operational terms, it is useful to view the various key steps in each phase as viewed from an instructional designer's perspective.

Analysis

- ◆ Frame the challenge, problem, or need into tangible action items.
- ◆ Determine if each is an instructional or non-instructional issue.
- ◆ Forward non-instructional items to appropriate resources for resolution.
- ◆ Evolve strategies for instructional issues.
- ◆ Perform the necessary analysis processes to gather data.
- ◆ Determine needed resources.
- ◆ Draft a budget and time line.
- ◆ Obtain sign-off.
- ◆ Evaluate all analysis elements.

Design

1. Draft a design plan as your blueprint for the project.
   - ◆ Rationale
   - ◆ Objectives
   - ◆ Population profile
   - ◆ Course description
   - ◆ Learner and facilitator prerequisites
   - ◆ Evaluation strategy
   - ◆ Deliverables
2. Evaluate all design elements.

Development

1. Draft the lesson plan.
   - ◆ Gaining attention
   - ◆ Direction
   - ◆ Recall
   - ◆ Content
   - ◆ Application feedback—level 1
   - ◆ Application feedback—level 2
   - ◆ Application feedback—level 3
   - ◆ Evaluation
   - ◆ Closure
2. Draft the materials (where applicable).
3. Draft online content (where applicable).
4. Pilot-test (as applicable).
5. Modify as necessary based on pilot testing evaluation.
6. Evaluate all development elements.

Implementation

1. Move project to active status.
2. Evaluate (Kirkpatrick levels 1–3):
   - ◆ Reaction
   - ◆ Learning
   - ◆ Behavior
3. Modify as necessary based on evaluation.
4. Evaluate all implementation elements.

Evaluation

1. Review all five ADDIE elements continuously.
2. Revise evaluation process as necessary.

Case Study—The ADDIE Model at Work

This case study is drawn from an actual utilization of the ADDIE model for a large corporation in the service industry. It demonstrates the ways in which an instructional designer works through the ADDIE elements to meet a training need within the corporation.

As a background, this organization provides information technology solutions for the retail environment. The instructional designer was tasked by senior managers to create a course for installers, support technicians, marketing staff, and hardware technicians to ensure that all these staff functions provide the best possible customer support to the end user.

As is the case with many training programs in large organizations, the instructional designer is not a SME in any of the content areas targeted in this set of courses.

Analysis

To get started, our designer needed to gather some very basic analysis questions. As with all ISD projects, analysis is the first element and is critical to the success of the project. These questions needed answers:

- ◆ Why do we need this course?
- ◆ What makes this content so different from what already exists that it requires a new course?
- ◆ What information needs to be covered in the course?

To gather the needed data, our designer used face-to-face interviews to gather information that would be relevant in the course. She interviewed support technicians (software and hardware), installation technicians, hardware technical writers, members of the hardware research and development department, and the director of hardware services to establish what information is necessary for a technician in the field. She also read support cases to see what some of the major problem areas were. As a result of these interviews, she concluded that the following topics should be included in the course:

- ◆ basic overview of the products
- ◆ how this software and hardware are different from others
- ◆ basic knowledge of all components (parts identification)
- ◆ what parts are replaceable
- ◆ how to install the replacement parts
- ◆ how to convert one model to the newer model
- ◆ how to use some basic troubleshooting techniques.

Design

Once the basic analysis was performed, our designer moved on to the design element or blueprinting stage of ISD. She wrote terminal objectives for the course. The design took into account the need to integrate evaluation later in the development. When the objectives were completed, our designer had SMEs review them and provide feedback; and then our designer modified the objectives as necessary.

From the objectives, she determined that the best delivery method for instruction would be an instructor-led course with extensive hands-on exercises. Our designer created an organizational chart (similar to a course or topic map) so that she had a graphical representation of the topics and subtopics to be discussed. This helped her group and link different topics to one another. It also allowed her to create the necessary enabling objectives.

Development

Producing materials and pilot testing are the most important elements of the development phase of ISD. For developing this course, our designer followed the nine events of instruction, which Gagne developed as a sequence for lesson plan design. Our designer also worked with her SMEs to ensure that the material she was creating was accurate.

At this point our designer was becoming more knowledgeable about the hardware and was actually able to identify, remove, and replace all of the replaceable parts herself. While she was working on the product, she and other staff members used a digital camera to photograph the different components. They used these photographs for a parts identification job aid on the company's website.

Before formal implementation of the course, a pilot class was held. The participants in the pilot class were new hires and members of the training department. The participants had no knowledge of the hardware. After completion of the two pilot offerings of the course, our designer convened a focus group to obtain feedback on the course. Their comments and suggestions were reviewed and implemented where feasible.

Implementation

Once pilot testing was completed and the necessary changes made to the course, materials were produced and the course was offered for implementation. At the completion of each course offering, level 1 and level 2 evaluations were given to course participants. These evaluations were reviewed by the training staff and managers, and corrective measures were taken as warranted.

Evaluation

At the conclusion of the first round of course implementation, our designer made several changes based on the course evaluations completed by the learners. The course received great reviews, and the learners commented on how well they learned from the hands-on activities. A final level 3 evaluation was distributed to learners and their supervisors six months after the course was offered to gauge whether the course had any effect on the ability of the company to meet customer needs. The data showed a positive effect on customer satisfaction as viewed from the perspective of the course participants.

While this is a very simple example of how the ADDIE model works, it gives you some background for the rest of the book as we go into much more detail on each element of the process.

Other ISD Models

There are probably as many informal ISD models as there are instructional designers, and that is the way it should be with ISD. Although many formal models exist for instructional designers to follow and learn from, each individual designer does things a little bit differently in the real world. No two projects evolve exactly the same way, and there have never been two instructional designers designing projects the same way. In fact, not every instructional designer uses the ADDIE model, but the five elements—analysis, design, development, implementation, and evaluation—should always be operational in instructional design.

As an instructional designer gains experience, the ISD elements combine in a way that works uniquely for him or her. Derivations of any model are necessary to meet different design strategies. Different designers write objectives differently, and no two surveys ever look exactly the same. Every designer eventually evolves to create a unique model of ISD based on the same fundamental ADDIE structure. It is not uncommon in some ISD models to see an additional level of analysis or evaluation or another element added to meet a specific design or organizational need. That it is why it is safe to say there are as many ISD models as there are instructional designers.

The cardinal rule of ISD is to never leave out analysis and evaluation, the two most commonly overlooked and abused elements of the model. Projects without analysis and evaluation can be spotted quickly because (1) they seldom work and (2) no one ever really figures out why they failed.

Characteristics of a Well-Designed Program

The saying that hard work is usually disguised as luck resonates in training. The most successful training programs have the appearance of being effortlessly designed and delivered. The content is appropriate for the audience, there is just enough material to cover in the time allowed, participants are able to meet the objectives, and evaluations ensure that the course design provides the desired results.

At the other extreme, a program that was put together with little planning or little thought about the desired results leaves learners confused, and the evaluations, if there are any, concentrate on nontraining issues like the comfort of the chairs or the cleanliness of the restrooms. Participants leave those programs wondering why they bothered to invest their time. The difference between these two situations typically is directly related to the time and expertise invested in the instructional design process. The evidence that a program has been well designed can be observed in the participants: They have learned.

In Conclusion

The ADDIE model of instructional design encompasses all of the elements necessary for professional and effective curriculum development. Within the simple framework of analysis, design, development, implementation, and evaluation are found all of the required elements to provide instructional design solutions for any training and education challenge—from classroom courses to online training programs for multinational organizations.

Discussion Questions

1. Do you think that following a model while designing a course is a good idea?
2. Would you add or subtract any elements to the ADDIE model?
3. How do you know when a course has been designed well?

◆ Section II

ADDIE Elements

Chapter 4

Analysis

Chapter Objectives

At the conclusion of this chapter, you should be able to

- ◆ define the analysis process using the ADDIE model
- ◆ determine the difference between training and nontraining problems
- ◆ list three data-gathering steps
- ◆ identify the four levels of detail in task analysis
- ◆ describe three critical elements of a population analysis
- ◆ list at least three instructional methods and their uses.

Analysis Basics

The process of analysis is the foundation for any instructional design project. Although it is the most often neglected aspect of ISD, analysis is not an option for the successful designer. For a world full of reasons that sometimes border on irrational, analysis has to fight for the respect it deserves in instructional design. Analysis is often labeled as unnecessary, too expensive, or too time-consuming; yet to avoid or neglect the basics of analysis is to design at your own peril. Even the most seemingly obvious analysis questions relating to populations, goals, and resources never find voice and therefore become static and usually questionable constants in an instructional system.

The harsh reality that faces many designers is that even though ISD practitioners know the importance of analysis, a majority of clients and others outside the profession have very little interest in the process and even less inclination to allocate the resources of time and money necessary to do it correctly. That being said, analysis is almost always performed and usually by any means necessary, which often involves "borrowing" from other resources to gather the data needed.

In the analysis stage, instructional designers can never know too much. Curiosity is the first analysis skill that belongs in a designer's tool kit, where it will pay countless dividends. It is impossible to ask too many questions, and it is difficult to imagine starting a design project without the essential analysis completed.

Seven key questions require answers during analysis. By addressing each of these questions, instructional designers ensure that they gather all the data they are likely to need as they work their way through the ADDIE system. The questions also help designers check that they have focused on all the possible aspects of the course under consideration. In short, these questions serve as a reality check:

1. What is the need?
2. What is the root cause?
3. What are the goals of the training?
4. What information is needed, and how is it gathered?
5. How will the training be structured and organized?
6. How will the training be delivered?
7. When should training be revised?

The rest of this chapter hones in on each of these questions and highlights some common problems that instructional designers face.

What Is the Need?

Need is the gatekeeper for entry into analysis. If there is no need for the course, there is no need to perform an analysis. This relationship between need and analysis holds true even if a designer has been given an assignment to design a course and has no option except completing it with only two weeks' notice.

Many designers believe that training is the best solution to numerous problems in an organization. Experience shows, however, that some problems do not require training solutions. In fact, they are not training problems at all. For example, the staff at a company may not be communicating with one another. Although they send emails, blog, or tweet, these efforts are never seen by the intended people. Training will not help those employees improve their communications because the problem is not how to produce the message; it is about standardizing communication choices.

A range of issues exists that cannot be fixed with training. Other examples include low wages, miserable working conditions, and the lack of proper equipment. Undoubtedly, there are solutions for these issues, and performance improvement specialists can find ways to solve them. An instructional designer's role in an unhappy work situation should not include designing a course titled "My Boss Is Always Correct."

Designers must determine early on if a training intervention can remedy anything about an apparent problem. If they determine that a training solution is possible, they can move on to the next level of analysis. If they determine that training is not the solution, then they must recognize the reality and move to find other solutions.

The cardinal rule of the analysis element of ISD is this: Always determine that there is a training solution before providing one. Or, to shamelessly bend the Hippocratic Oath: Never do harm.

Not every need requires training. In the larger world of performance improvement, nontraining solutions are viable and can have a sizable impact; however, within instructional design, the gatekeeper function is critical regardless of the eventual solution. That function enables the designer to get the information needed to make an informed decision.

Typically, designers find that the type of training selected as a solution is based on a learner's lack of knowledge, skills, or abilities, or a combination of these elements. Training solutions are nearly always available for any performance need that falls within this group. Training does not offer solutions for wages, benefits, working conditions, organizational procedures, or personality conflicts.

What Is the Root Cause?

The first task for a designer is to identify the need and determine the root cause of any problems that may exist. Sometimes the need and root cause are relatively easy to uncover. At other times, they may take some digging to reveal. Designers must listen carefully to what they hear and use their logic filter to test each potential issue.

It is important to point out that even though a need appears to be instructional in nature, it might not be. That assessment might be made on the basis of symptoms and not the root cause of the problem. Just as in medicine, treating the symptoms may initially reduce the pain, but it seldom cures the illness.

Following are two situations in which training is not the solution:

◆ An office is displaying symptoms of discord that are interfering with normal work activities. After some analysis, it is determined that a new supervisor is not working out well with the group. Rather than dealing with the supervisor, management suggests that the training department offer some courses on attitude readjustment and team building. This intervention will not solve the problem because it does not touch the root cause—the supervisor.

◆ At another organization, an undercurrent of sexual harassment problems gained the attention of the executive director. Management expected violations within the organization to diminish or even disappear because of training, but following the training, reports of violations soared. Management blamed the training for the increase. The unexpected result of the training was the empowerment of workers who had experienced problems and now felt obligated to come forward with complaints. The root problem, though, was several individuals who did not see themselves as doing anything offensive.

Here are two situations in which training may be solutions:

◆ The partners at a law firm are upset about the sudden decline in the quality and quantity of their support staff's work. A senior partner investigates and learns that the office manager has recently upgraded the word-processing program. The new version is designed specifically for law offices and requires the staff to learn new computer commands. The office manager chose not to accept the initial training, which the supplier offered at a reduced rate at the time of purchase. The solution now is simple: to give software training to the staff. Unfortunately, the cost for training will be higher than if it had been ordered earlier. The firm is also paying a high cost in the diminished morale.

◆ A small, nonprofit group has a yearly fund-raising drive to support its community-based programs. This year the group decided to move from door-to-door solicitation to phone solicitation. Donations are off by more than 30 percent, and the board of directors is livid! The executive director has followed the advice of a consulting firm that has assisted a number of for-profit organizations to improve their sales. Unfortunately, the nonprofit group tried to save money by using older volunteers who have no phone solicitation experience and were having trouble reading the calling scripts that were printed in small type. Several approaches could solve this difficulty. A role-playing training class for the volunteers might help them improve their skills in making calls.

What Are the Goals of the Training?

Anyone who is going to design a training project must know the rationale for the project. The rationale is a mission statement that clearly states the project's reason for existing. It is the heart and soul of the work to be done. The place to start is with the sponsoring department, manager, organization, or client, who can communicate the goals to the designer. Designers need to verify or correct assumptions that may exist. It is important to ask questions such as, What does success for this project mean to you? and When will you be happy with this project?

The aim is to get to the bottom of the motivational issues, because things that may seem trivial to the designer may be a major issue in a project. With projects for internal clients, designers should be sure the results match the unit's goals as well as the goals of the larger organization. By attending to both groups, designers will protect themselves from getting caught in the crossfire if the project does not resonate with the larger organizational goals.

Sometimes the goals of the sponsor and the reality of the content do not make sense, and the designer must step back and find out why. For example, it is not uncommon for an organization to want to use a new technology for training in an effort to look current with the trends in a certain industry although analysis may show that the learners do not need or want a technology-based solution. In this case, the goals of the organization and the reality of the situation do not match. On those occasions, someone may be operating under a hidden and self-interested agenda. Instructional designers must be alert to the possibility that they may discover problems like these in the populations they serve:

◆ Career boosting is usually framed by someone whose real interest is in showcasing his or her contribution to management. Evidence that career boosting is at work on a project is often in design that is heavy on production values and low on instructional design values. Training designed for show can often backfire when the cost to produce unnecessary or ineffective training is discovered.

◆ Getting-even training is discovered when the training goals seem to be, "We'll show them how to…" or "They won't do that to us again!"

◆ Propaganda training is always designed to send a message to someone. Evidence is that the message is more important than the behavioral objective.

Sound goals designers are likely to see might include an increase of sales by a certain percentage or reduction in the number of mistakes being generated by the implementation of a new software package in an organization.

What Information Is Needed, and How Is It Gathered?

The first three questions helped instructional designers determine that training can address the need and is consistent with individual and organizational goals. Now it is necessary to obtain information in both subject matter and nonsubject matter areas.

Subject matter is the heart of the project, but nonsubject matter is the soul. Information on both will form the basis for the design plan. This book will look at design plans in much more detail in the next chapter.

The nonsubject matter information needed for the design plan includes the rationale for the course (usually described as the goals for the training), population data, course structure, and deliverables. The subject matter information eventually ends up as objectives, evaluation strategies, facilitator prerequisites, and learner prerequisites.

The Population Analysis Process

Having precise knowledge of a population of learners for a design project is most often key in making critical decisions related to objectives, delivery modalities, and evaluations as well as myriad other possible questions that can arise in the design process. Gathering data and analyzing populations of learners require skills that might seem intuitive on the surface but require countless hours of practice to perfect. The subtleties associated with populations are numerous and the variations within each population are countless.

Each population is unique, and the biggest mistake designers make in this area is to ignore this process. You must analyze the population, even if that only means verifying the data that you have been given or seeking clarification in areas that seem conflicted. Populations are complex, and every variable experienced in any individual or group of people has the potential to be present in any population analyzed.

What a Population Analysis Tells a Designer

Population analysis is distinctly different from other types of analysis because the focus is on the relationship between the individual and the project being designed. This being the case, we look for specific types of data that give us keys to this relationship. For example, we need to know the present level of content mastery in a population, the relationship between that mastery and the proposed content, and the best way to implement the content with a specific population. In some projects, however, that is only the beginning. We may need to know about motivation, language competency, cultural norms, learning styles, and numerous other variables.

Many non-designers associated with a project often say that there is very little value in performing a population analysis unless there is a recognized set of issues that exists within a population. Without taking the time to check, there is no way for a designer to discover, acknowledge, and address population variables. Designing a course in workplace communications would suggest that a careful look at the target population is necessary since the content relates directly to a population's ability to communicate with each other. But the same issues can exist in a new employee orientation or a course in retirement planning within an organization and might be ignored because the importance of population data isn't as obvious.

There are certain basic sets of data that designers need to gather and consider as they review a population. The order of importance for these is different for each project and may actually change during the design process, depending on the environment and volatility of the content or design.

Content Mastery

Designers must be able to determine the anticipated level of content mastery for a population at the start of a course. This is easy if there is no minimum level of mastery required for participating in a course, but that is seldom the reality. Even open-enrollment or community participation courses have some expectation for mastery, even if it is a seemingly obvious element like basic language skills or literacy at a certain grade level.

In some cases, it will be necessary to actually perform a skills analysis to determine content mastery in a specific population. In other situations, it may be acceptable to review general population data available through numerous sources.

In determining mastery, tools like the content mastery continuum may prove valuable. You can review that process in chapter 15.

Demographics

We are all familiar with demographic data sets such as age, gender, and educational achievement level. There are times when more sophisticated demographic data is useful, and gathering this data requires a systematic approach to analysis. A designer needs to determine what, if any, demographic variable may affect course design.

There are times when population members may consider data privileged or sensitive. When you ask about marital status, income, religious affiliation, criminal history, bankruptcy, and similar topics, you may have difficulty gathering accurate data for analysis. There are times when this data is available from other sources, but you must always honor any legal or ethical concerns and restrictions. HIPAA (Health Insurance Portability and Accountability Act) and FERPA (Family

Educational Rights and Privacy Act) are but two of the federal laws that regulate the gathering and handling of data, and as a designer you must always honor those restrictions.

Motivation and Attitude

Determining how a population views a content area or its participation in a course is almost always invaluable information for an instructional designer. With so much training and education now considered mandatory, motivation and attitude play an increasingly larger role in course design.

If a course is in a content area that is considered personal or is something that is uncomfortable for a learner, a designer needs to know how a population will react to the learning environment and the content before the course is implemented. Diversity and workplace behavior are often content areas that require an attitude scan among the population to determine underlying issues. It is much easier to design in measures to neutralize or deal with issues within a course than it is to implement a course and then leave the facilitator with the responsibility for dealing with potential problems as they arise.

Language and Culture

In today's international populations, both within the community and at places of employment, it is considered standard ISD practice to determine if language or cultural variations will affect a specific population of learners. This is also the case when programs are being designed and implemented for a language or culture different than the designer's native language and culture. Very simple, but often missed, issues related to translation and its effect on the timing of a course are examples. Simultaneous translation takes less time than consecutive translation, so a course that lasts four hours can easily take six or more hours if consecutive instead of simultaneous translation is used.

A cultural read on a population often addresses issues related to respect and familiarity for culture differences within the population. No designer wants to make a simple mistake in materials or interaction that violates cultural norms within a population. This isn't about being politically correct. It is about making sure that differences are recognized and addressed within a population to ensure that no barriers are created to interfere with a program's success.

Implementation Preferences

As every instructional designer knows, populations generally have varying views on how they want to receive instruction. Some learners want to be online while others prefer the classroom. A small minority may want to have synchronous online learning while a majority think "anytime, anyplace" better suits their available time and opt for asynchronous online learning when given an option.

While some design environments are project or organizationally limited to one implementation vehicle or another, others are not, and a population analysis is generally the way to determine preferences. In some instances, analysis results defy conventional logic and provide designers with data that can literally save a project by implementing in a way that is most appealing to a majority of a population. For example, a very high-tech, corporate population was thought to prefer online learning because they worked in a high-tech environment. Delivery was relatively simple and cost-effective given the technology already in place for online course delivery. A population analysis, however, showed that this population was relatively bored with using technology for this purpose and wanted the opportunity to learn with others in a classroom environment. The end product was a traditional facilitator-led series of courses that were very well received and actually proved to be significantly less expensive to produce and implement. Without the population analysis, the project could have run into significant motivational issues that would have negated most of the potential for success.

Technology and Distance Learning Acceptance and Utilization

While distance learning is making inroads into the training and education community, it is not the answer for all populations and courses. As the previous example shows, not even high-tech populations necessarily want distance learning options for training.

While the ISD process doesn't have an opinion on how a course is implemented, it certainly has a role in determining what works best for a specific population and content area. The process of determining this fit starts with a population analysis that includes gathering data related to distance learning attitudes and access issues.

Attitudinal data can easily be obtained that relates to preferences in learning implementation. Important questions related to when and where the training takes place must relate directly to the options available. If, in an office environment, learners are required to take a course during work hours, they may prefer a classroom setting. If they are expected to take a course on their own time, they may well prefer an online option. Be sure to run the entire spectrum of options to accurately measure population preferences

Any and All Other Relevant Population Data

One thing is for certain: There is something unique about each population. Sometimes these are minor elements that have no real bearing on a project's future, and other times the smallest points will have a major impact. It is also not unheard of for things to change or suddenly appear in a population as a project moves through design and development. A diligent designer will continuously scan the population for anything that might have been overlooked or ignored in the analysis process.

How to Conduct a Population Profile

It is important early in the population analysis process to establish which issues may influence the project's success. A simple rubric works fine for this step. For each element that may have an effect, the designer will say whether or not it could affect the outcome of the project, why, and whether he or she can do anything about it.

The designer should analyze each of these issues with one question in mind: Can this element affect the outcome of this project? For each element, the designer would ask if it has the potential to cause success or failure. Motivation and incentive issues alone can sink a really well-designed training project if they have not been taken into account. If the answer is yes, it can cause success or failure, the designer must address why, and then what he or she is going to do about it.

Conducting a population analysis can be a complex undertaking, but there are some very simple steps any designer can follow to ensure at least a basic profile of any population.

First, gather and review the demographics of the target population.

Demographics are the nuts and bolts of a population, and there is little in the way of opinion-based data in this section of an analysis. The types of demographic data you need are based on the design, but generally they include census-like data that relates to age, gender, ethnicity, culture, income, location, education, and other related variables. Often this data is included in a survey given to the population to complete. This data is generally easily obtained, but there are times when one or more of these data areas are considered either too personal, too invasive, or unnecessary by the population and you may have to gather data either by a secondary source like organizational or regional data or by estimating as best you can. There are times when the process of gathering this data itself can be considered invasive by a population, and in the best interests of process you may decide to forgo the formal data collection process and replace it with a more observational approach.

Second, gather data related to attitudes, values, and opinions.

Knowing how a population feels about a certain content area or situation is sometimes vital data in a population analysis. If you are working on a course for a troubled workforce, knowing why population members feel a certain way is key to building a course-based solution. There are design projects that will sink or swim based on this data, and being able to gather it is critical to project success. In other populations and design projects this attitudinal information has limited value. For example, do you really care if a technician enjoys replacing a part in a sophisticated piece of electronic equipment if there is no viable option for making it more enjoyable?

There are various methods available to gather this information, including surveys, interviews, and focus groups. There is a tendency to find more affective-based data in the more personal and one-on-one analysis methods of interview and focus group. Surveys (usually anonymous) are of value for larger populations or where the subject is less personal or closely held.

Third, gather everything else.

A pro-level instructional designer is always looking for that extra data set that will provide a key bit of information that will add value to the analysis process. Many times these moments are unexpected, unsolicited, and yet enormously important to the design process. It is not unusual for a designer to learn about something critical to a design based on an overheard conversation or quick review of an organizational newsletter or publication. Don't be afraid to gather every bit of information that comes your way and review it for hidden nuggets of data.

Fourth, consider issues of the cultural environment.

If you are working on a design project for a population that is unfamiliar to you or is geographically or culturally distant from your experience, pay special attention to the environment in which the population resides. Many times these seemingly small points of data are ignored or rejected because they are not within the functional comfort zone of the designer. As an example, recently it was important to analyze differences that would not normally be an issue for designers in a Western country since the project was to be implemented in another continent and assumed knowledge of analysis needs was not enough to make this project a success. Some of the factors designers had to consider included:

- ◆ *Religious influence:* It was important that designers consider prayer times and other religious ceremonies that might conflict with training times.
- ◆ *Gender interaction:* Traditional gender roles might create challenges in designing group activities, including role-play exercises.
- ◆ *Attendance and timing issues:* Many countries are more polychronic (time is more fluid) than the Western monochromic attitude that expects extreme punctuality.

◆ *Evaluation techniques:* Some populations might be hesitant to offer opinions or criticism of one another or to question a facilitator.

◆ *Appropriate materials:* Designers must consider participants' views about how materials represent them, especially graphic representations. The manner of dress and types of activities shown in materials must be acceptable to the target population.

◆ *Religious/cultural schedules:* In many areas of the world, the normal workweek is not Monday to Friday. Variables like this occur within the individual countries and populations represented in a typical cohort of learners. It is also important not to schedule training during religious holidays.

Ultimately this list led to a comprehensive training project that reflected the needs of the population and helped ensure a good start to the design plan. It is important that all the elements in a population study have an effect on the design.

Developing Surveys

Every instructional designer uses surveys; how designers use them can determine success or failure. How questions are asked is the key. Open-ended questions lead to open-ended answers, but for *quantifiable data,* designers must ask quantifiable questions and supply specific ranges of answers. For example, a designer who wants to ask 100 workers about their ability to use a specific software package might ask either of these questions:

◆ How well can you use the software?
◆ How well can you use the software? (a) very well, (b) know most of the commands I need, (c) struggle with some commands, (d) not very well, (e) not at all.

In the first example, the designer will get a range of answers that cannot be easily compared to each other or a standard from which to start designing. The designer who asks the second question will be able to compute percentages and use those data to design the course based on quantifiable data. If 50 percent say they know the software very well and 20 percent say not very well, the designer can eliminate the top 50 percent and concentrate on the bottom 50 percent who need skill enhancement.

Rating questions also are useful to providing insight into content. For example, a designer might ask: "How do you rate your ability to perform the following functions using the software: Mail merge (a) flawlessly, (b) few problems, (c) many problems, (d) cannot use it at all." The designer would then ask about all of the commands or skills that might be considered content in the course. The designer will build the basis of the content for the course as he or she works through the questions. This same process works for almost any skill-based analysis.

For sampling *attitudes,* designers can also turn to surveys and change the style of questions to some degree. In the case of a workplace in chaos, the questions might be:

◆ How would you rate the number of interpersonal problems in the office? (a) no problems, (b) some minor problems, (c) many problems, (d) nothing but problems.

◆ In your opinion, what is the atmosphere like in the office? (a) no tension, (b) some tension, (c) very tense, (d) chaotic.

How Will the Training Be Structured and Organized?

Task analysis is the grandparent of all analysis methods. It involves the process of breaking down a job or assignment into each task associated with it to learn the skills and knowledge necessary to perform it. The data gathered in this process assist the designer in building the structure of the project, including instructional methods and media. They also tell how best to organize objectives and evaluations in a logical continuum from beginning to end.

Task analysis is something every instructional designer does, and it can be used for a variety of situations. Jobs, skills, procedures, processes, and of course tasks are usually best analyzed in this manner. Task analysis is the first step for an instructional designer who needs to replicate anything that involves human interaction in a series of steps. An instructional designer would perform a task analysis to be sure a lesson covers every step a person needs to know in order to perform the job, skill, procedure, process, or task.

Conducting a Task Analysis

Even though it is such a fundamental tool of the instructional designer, task analysis is often done poorly or given little preparation time. In fact, it is not as simple as one might assume. Four levels of detail exist in a task analysis: job, task, skill, and subskill.

Some instructional designers spend most of their professional lives working in situations that require them to follow technical task-analysis procedures. Imagine trying to perform a task analysis on a job like that of manager of an energy-producing nuclear reactor. That job involves numerous tasks that must

---

Task Analysis Examples

Job: air traffic controller
    Task: giving an airplane clearance to land at an airport
    Skills: monitoring a number of data screens and looking out the window of
    the tower
    Subskill: checking the radar screen for possible problems.

Job: vice president of sales
    Task: monthly reporting
    Skills: gathering data, writing reports, and so forth
    Subskill: accessing the organization's spreadsheets and locating the sales figures.

---

be replicated exactly the way they are engineered because a misstep in the task analysis could put people's lives in jeopardy. Consider what would happen if a task analysis missed a key step in a safety procedure. As a result of that omission, employees might not receive training for a specific problem that might occur. No training probably means diminished effectiveness in dealing with the problem.

Several steps are vitally important in task analysis from the perspective of a designer:

1. *Define the target of the analysis:* With whom are you going to work? What titles or responsibilities do you want to analyze?
2. *Choose the methodology:* Will you use task analysis, focus groups, or other methods of analysis?
3. *Select the analysis subjects:* Choose the best candidates for analysis. Typically, these are the people who actually do the work and are considered the best at it. It helps to work with several individuals who are struggling with a task so designers can see why they are having trouble.

Task Analysis Field Visit

One of the best ways to learn the art of task analysis is to go into the real world and give it a try. This isn't nearly as difficult as it may seem at first. Designers actually perform task analysis many times a day without thinking about it. A good example might be standing in line to use an unfamiliar automated teller machine. As people work their way up the line, they are actually doing task analysis as they watch those in front operate the machine. Each time one person performs an operation, people in line are observing and remembering how it is done. People in line—those analyzing—note when someone makes a mistake and remember to avoid those same errors.

How Will the Training Be Delivered?

Instructional designers need to determine the distribution methods and instructional methods they will be working with early in their planning, sometimes before really starting the project. It is essential that these two elements be in place before designers get too involved with the design phase.

Possible Instructional Methods

Instructional designers make choices that determine how learners interact with the subject matter. The designer's tool of matching innovative distribution methods and instructional methods is important. Instructional methods are techniques that designers use to link objectives with learners. Lectures, group discussions, and case studies all serve as the link between the learner and the subject matter, much the same way as a book or webpage links information with the end user. Distribution methods are the ways designers deliver the instructional methods. Proper matching of distribution and instructional methods and platforms also saves time and energy, for both the designer and the learner.

These are some of the more frequently used instructional methods:

- ◆ *Lecture:* With few exceptions, instructional designers should only use lectures in combination with other methods. They might use them alone if they have an inspirational facilitator and want to inspire learners. Otherwise, learners will be fighting back yawns and hunger pains while a facilitator is lecturing. With lectures, it is important to have in place the design elements of clear time limits as well as liberal use of visuals or other stimulators.
- ◆ *Role-play:* In role-plays, learners enact the roles of people placed in various situations in an effort to closely match the training with the real world. Role-plays are a great way of placing learners in the action of solving a problem or practicing a skill. Instructional designers must be mindful of any issues that could cause problems if they use role-playing with a group of introverts or a population facing some physical or emotional challenges. Designers must take the time to prepare both the role and scenario descriptions and very precise instructions to both learners and facilitators.
- ◆ *Case study:* This method moves the learner up the cognitive ladder and requires decisions, either in a group or singly. Case studies are great ways to provide instruction in cognitive skills like negotiating, facilitating, reasoning, and constructing solutions. Instructional designers must be careful to ensure that the cases are relevant to their learners. If the cases are out of

the learners' contextual framework, they are not likely to hold the learners' interest. It is vitally important that the instructor provides complete case studies, not just bits and pieces of a case. Incomplete information can easily turn a case intended to illustrate a marketing challenge into a case solved by the company giving employees two weeks of additional vacation every year. For example, a case study might say that employees were working without any days off, but it might fail to mention that the extra work was because the office was being moved to another building. Without providing complete information, readers may be sympathetic to the workers and want to give them extra vacation.

◆ *Simulations:* Practice, practice, and more practice. Simulation is one of the best methods for getting learners to practice a skill, process, task, or procedure. It is also great for psychomotor skills. Simulations are the process of performing a task in a safe environment. They are especially helpful for dangerous or expensive tasks. Psychomotor objectives are exercised in simulations because there is no chance of damaging expensive equipment or injuring a participant in a dangerous procedure.

◆ *Gaming:* Gaming is the process of placing participants in the position of having multiple choices to make in an exercise that borders on real life but provides the safety of a simulation. Just as video games simulate some level of reality, gaming provides the same safe environment without subjecting participants to the dangers of actually performing a task. Some of the best gaming is sophisticated and reaches the limits of technology. Many military applications are right at the corner of reality and surrealism.

◆ *Critical incident:* This method is used in many training areas that challenge the ability of a learner to react quickly to a problem. Essentially, this is a version of a case study, but it leaves out some of the key data. Airline pilots are subjected to critical incident methods when they simulate flights that develop problems. The extensive use of flight data recorders has allowed the advancement of this method in transportation training.

◆ *Drill:* Keep doing it, doing it, doing it. Drills are used extensively in computer-based training. For example, many programs require learners to enter words or numbers numerous times to complete a sentence or math problem.

◆ *Job aid:* This training method pays great dividends in many projects. Job aids are any material that workers keep at hand for easy reference, such as a printed form, cheat sheet, or procedures manual, that contains information on a concept or skill. Since the human memory is often unreliable, it is useful to have something in hand that supports the concept or skill involved. Job aids, many times, can stand on their own and not require any class or technology time to implement.

◆ *Critique:* This is a modified case study approach that requires determining the strengths and weaknesses of a situation or process, then finding a solution. An annual review by a boss is a valid instructional method.

◆ *Discussion:* In this context, discussion is directed, follows another activity, and creates the environment for interactivity. The discussions may be large group, small group, buzz groups, or teams. Generally, the discussion should not involve groups larger than 25 or 30 learners. If size is an issue, the group should be broken down into workable chunks. It is important that instructional designers prepare both the facilitator and the learners before any discussion starts so they know what they will be discussing and why. Without direction or preparation, the group may wander off the subject.

◆ *In-basket:* Learners participate by working through a pile of data sitting in front of them, usually on a desk. They have to make decisions about each item, and the results offer a snapshot of their ability to solve problems. This method usually incorporates a degree of role-play and case-study methods.

◆ *On-the-job training:* On-the-job training (OJT) is probably the most often used instructional method. Some organizations realize they are using it, but others—those that have an employee probation period—may not realize they're using it. OJT is intended to be mentoring in its purest form. Instructional designers must ensure that this method does not preclude use of others.

◆ *Brainstorming:* This method asks learners to build experience into creativity by developing ideas on a specific subject with other colleagues. It can be tough to pull off and sometimes even tougher to design because it is free-wheeling. Brainstorming sessions should never last more than 10 minutes, and facilitators should be given enough ideas for refocusing if the group becomes lethargic. Designers need to accept the fact that brainstorming may backfire on the facilitator and that these sessions have the potential to have a negative effect on the success of the project if the process bogs down in political or emotional responses. For example, a group that is working to find new ideas for a marketing campaign may end up blaming engineering for never having the right product available when the market peaks. It becomes important, therefore, that a facilitator be prepared to nudge the group back on track and away from a negative ending.

Other methods that are related directly to technology are computer-based training, multimedia, interactive TV, teleconferencing, groupware, virtual reality, and employee performance support systems (EPSSs).

Instructional Methods to Avoid

There are at least four instructional methods to avoid:

- *Technology regardless of effectiveness:* This is a common temptation when a new technology becomes popular and there is very little reason to support it being used in training or education. Always ask yourself the design question, Does this support learning?
- *Undirected groups:* This method is usually little more than groups discussing a topic or subject matter with little or no direction by a facilitator. It is typically used to kill time and offers little, if any, instructional value.
- *Unguided missile:* This seldom-used method usually begins with this statement from the facilitator at a training session: "Now, let's decide what we are going to do today." Although it may appear that there is a positive in getting group consensus for objectives, the method is an abandonment of instructional principles.
- *Theory tantrums:* Instructors must not dwell on theory. Training courses can only stand the smallest bits of theory when they substantiate a point or set the groundwork for something that follows. Always turn theory into practice.

Types of Distribution Methods

A number of distribution methods are widely used for training. The ones presented here are just a starting point for the discussion:

- *Captive audience:* Otherwise known as *classroom training,* this is the most common way to administer training. It consists of one or more learners with one or more facilitators in a single location using no technologies.
- *Technology-enhanced:* This is the name for training that makes use of an overhead, slide projector, or laptop and computer projector. One or more technologies assist in the implementation of the course.
- *Technology-facilitated:* This is what is commonly referred to by several hundred different terms such as *multimedia, computer-based training (CBT), e-learning,* and *virtual reality.* This platform is delivered with the technology,

learner, and perhaps a facilitator in one location with the technology serving the dominant role in facilitation.

◆ *Distance learning:* This term describes the method in which learners are at one or more different physical locations than the source of the instruction. Teleconferencing is an example of distance learning.

◆ *Distributed learning:* Home study courses are an example of this method. Training is distributed by a process, such as mail, that is not related to the implementation.

Other distribution methods include cable television, CD-ROM, email, extranets, Internet, intranets, local area networks (LANs), satellite television, simulators, voicemail, wide area networks (WANs), and the World Wide Web.

Learning technologies may be *synchronous* or *asynchronous.* Synchronous learning assumes that the learning and the facilitation take place at the same time. A good example is a chat room on the Internet. Everyone is participating in real time, and learners are usually expected to participate at a set time, much as a regular training course. Asynchronous training allows late sleepers and night owls to participate in training. Learners have a choice of when they participate as one benefit of the technology. Learning is sometimes implemented as an email system or a forum on a computer server.

When Should Training Be Revised?

Since the inception of the atomic age, most of us have become familiar with the term *half-life.* It refers to how long half of the atoms in a radioactive substance will continue to emit radiation before they disintegrate. It has also taken on a more cultural meaning. For instructional designers, the term refers to a period of validity. In some topic areas, the useful life of the data is measured in centuries. In others, it can literally be measured in seconds or minutes. In instructional design, half-life means the time it takes for a noticeable or significant change in data to take place.

It is important to note that this does not apply to all of the data becoming useless, but only enough of it to render the training suspect or dated. It may only take one incorrect element of the subject matter to ruin weeks of work by a designer. This obsolescence is particularly noticeable in computer- and web-based instruction. It is not uncommon for the design project to outlast the technology. A designer may, for example, design a computer-based training project on the basis of a certain hardware and software platform that could easily be at least a generation old when it is implemented.

To prevent this technology advancement from affecting a design, designers should ask the following data-decay rating questions for each element of the project that may be affected. Respond with a rating from 0 to 5 (lowest to highest):

- ◆ How critical is the data to the success of the training?
- ◆ How likely is it that the data will change?
- ◆ How easy is it to update data internally?
- ◆ Can learners or trainers easily obtain updated data?

If the analysis of the decay rating elements ends up being near the low end of the scale, designers should consider a process that allows for updating. This can be as easy as providing a webpage for updated information or distributing data sheets as necessary. In either case, designers should not assume that a completed project will rest comfortably on the information provided, unless they have determined that to be the case.

Common Problems and Solutions

Knowing some of the problems that are frequently encountered in ISD can help designers avoid them—or fix them early in the process.

Too Much or Too Little Content

Instructional designers rarely have the luxury of exactly matching the amount of content with the time available for implementation. It is common for designers to have three days of content for a two-hour implementation requirement or 20 minutes of content for an eight-hour window. The first consideration is to review chapter 17 on criticality. This is the most thorough way to determine content choices.

If time or budget doesn't allow for a formal criticality review, another effective way to solve the "too much content" issue is for the designer to call a meeting of all stakeholders in the training and marshal all the facts and data possible about the training. At the meeting, the designer should take the following steps toward a consensus decision on the content:

1. Cluster the data into topic areas.
2. Rank-order the topic areas.
3. Assign priorities to the data within each topic area.
4. Decide which topics and subtopics cannot be eliminated.
5. Review all topics and subtopics for redundancy.
6. Combine and eliminate subtopics as necessary.

7. Estimate timing on the topic areas and on each subtopic.

8. Map out a project plan and outline each topic with the subtopics underneath them.

9. Delineate the topics and subtopics with time indications so that it is obvious which ones will remain using different options.

If too little content remains, designers should review what they have to make sure they aren't missing something. If nothing is missing, they should try breaking down the topics into smaller chunks to see if it is possible to include more. It may also be possible to shorten the implementation time. It is never a good idea to waste a learner's time. Everyone can tell when instructors are stretching content. Designers need to offer realistic expectations for keeping this problem from surfacing.

When Training Is Mandated

Mandated training is an exception to the rules for both too much and too little information. Designers often have little leeway in designing around obvious mismatches. Designers should think about these things before they move to the design stage:

- ◆ Have you really determined the problem, gap, or need?
- ◆ Have you determined if it is training or nontraining?
- ◆ Have you gathered data?
- ◆ Have you considered using one or all of these analysis methods to gather data: focus group, surveys, task analysis, SME group?
- ◆ Who are your SMEs?
- ◆ What are the constraints and resources?
- ◆ Have you determined all of the organizational needs?
- ◆ Have you reviewed your distribution and instructional methods?
- ◆ Do you know the half-life of your content?
- ◆ Do you have too much or too little content?

In Conclusion

In this chapter, you have learned about the analysis stage of instructional systems design. During analysis, designers must determine the answers to seven crucial questions. They must determine the need for instructional design and decide whether training is the right intervention for responding to that need. Their analyses require them to explore the goals of the training and to gather information from population analyses, focus groups, surveys, and other sources. During this stage, they will conduct task analyses, which will help them to formulate the structure of their projects, and they will consider which instructional methods make sense. Before they begin designing a project, designers must also consider whether it is likely to be dated. Analysis requires a broad look ahead.

Discussion Questions

1. Why do you think analysis is so often ignored in the instructional design process?
2. What is the best way for a designer to determine the best implementation strategy for a specific course?
3. While conducting a population analysis for a new project, you discover that your data differs sharply from the antidotal information given to you by your client. What do you do?
4. Given the sensitive nature of gathering personal data, what do you think are acceptable areas to ask questions during a population analysis relating to demographics?

Chapter 5

Design

Chapter Objectives

At the conclusion of this chapter, you should be able to

- ◆ describe the design phase of the ISD process
- ◆ list at least three of the key roles the design phase plays in a typical ISD project.

The design element of the ISD process contains the majority of the work in most projects. By the same token, and sometimes confusing, many of the separate components of the instructional design process occur in the other four elements and are simply managed by the design function.

Using a systems approach, a diagram of the process looks like figure 5.1. The ISD process is design-centered, and each element of the system is managed by the design function. Each project will have a somewhat different delegation of the process and product, which will affect the work done in each element. However, what never changes is the control that the design function carries on the other elements in the process.

This centralization of the instructional design process evolved from the coordinating and managing role of the instructional designer in the process of curriculum development. This becomes obvious if you attempt to allow analysis, development, implementation, or evaluation to have the controlling interest in the process. All are

Figure 5.1. Systems Approach to the ISD Process

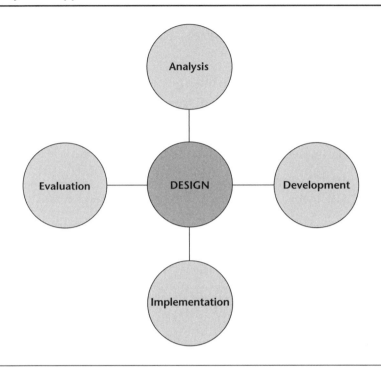

important, but a single function needs to have ultimate authority and responsibility. This places the design function and the instructional designer in the central coordinating role.

Design Element Functions

If you agree that the design function in the ADDIE model is the center of the process, then it is easy to say that everything must flow through design at one point or another, and that is certainly true in most situations. Sometimes it is extremely important to visualize the design function in a project management context to the degree that design requires coordination and staging of assets. Without at least a conceptual foundation of coordination and timing, design loses it value as the nucleus of ISD. This is true if a designer works alone in a project or works with a team of many designers and SMEs—it all requires the same processes.

General functions within the design element include:

◆ coordination of analysis, development, and evaluation processes
◆ centralized control and staging of assets, including design staff, development staff, and SMEs

- ◆ writing design plans
- ◆ writing lesson plans
- ◆ writing objectives
- ◆ writing evaluation tasks
- ◆ coordination between and among affiliate design project interests, including clients, sponsors, and other controlling interests
- ◆ quality control of all processes and products
- ◆ pilot testing coordination
- ◆ design and implementation of analysis and evaluation instruments.

Another critical aspect of the design phase is the somewhat subtle art of providing leadership throughout the process. There are a number of analogies that might fit for this key design role, but the most obvious is the traffic cop at the busy intersection. From every direction arrive challenges and decisions that must be addressed, sometimes with very little time for reflection. The designer-leader role shows itself most prominently when the fog is thickest, and the depth of a great instructional design is often tested at these moments. This is where a systems approach pays off handily as the emotion of key decisions is banished to the periphery as the logic of the choices sets in and becomes obvious.

There are very few designers that are not leaders too, and this is the real strength of the design process. In this phase the decisions are those relating to choices within a range of possibilities. In course delivery it might be a choice between online and blended, and choosing content is aided by criticality and other ISD tools. The seasoned designer in this environment facilitates decisions and "designs" within the boundaries of the data and choices. In ADDIE, the design phase is central to project success and the chief design goal of learner mastery. The design phase of the ADDIE ISD model is the most important element of the process. It is the central coordination and decision point within instructional design.

In Conclusion

The design element of the ADDIE model is the nucleus of the entire instructional design process. This element directs the activities and processes in analysis, development, implementation, and evaluation. As figure 5.1 depicts, every aspect of ISD is controlled and influenced by the design element. That is the major reason that professionals in ISD are often generically termed *instructional designers*.

Discussion Questions

1. You have just been given the responsibility for the design phase of a large training project. Where do you start?
2. How might the instructional designer provide leadership through the design phase in particular?

Chapter 6

Development

Chapter Objectives

At the conclusion of this chapter, you should be able to

- ◆ define the development phase of ISD
- ◆ list several aspects of development that require reviewing when developing materials
- ◆ give several reasons why pilot testing is essential when designing a curriculum
- ◆ describe why a train-the-trainer course may be necessary
- ◆ list several things to consider when designing a train-the-trainer course.

The *development phase* of ISD is the link that connects the design process with the implementation of a project. Plans and prototypes move to realization as the designer moves materials to a final draft stage. Additionally, online courses are placed in course shells, programmers code technology-based projects, graphic artists produce artwork, and every conceivable deliverable relating to the final product is either prepared or reviewed.

As the buffer between design and implementation, development necessitates that the instructional designer carefully monitor the process elements. It can be exciting for instructional designers to work with a variety of different professionals, but it can also be hectic. Careful communication at this point pays dividends later.

One of the most rewarding aspects of the development phase for instructional designers is that they get to see all of the design plans coming to life. Manuals, videos, webpages, and a hundred different tangible deliverables finally take shape. There is usually a collective sigh of relief once this happens, and it is easy to see why.

The development phase allows designers to put the finishing touches on the observable deliverables for a project. It is also the best opportunity to do pilot testing before a project goes into implementation.

Look and Feel

Development presents many opportunities to make mistakes in training design and production. Everyone has opinions about the way materials should appear, and it can sometimes be hard to get general agreement about even the simplest things. Designers play an important role in finding consensus and working with all elements of a project.

The process of moving from draft materials to a nearly final product is crucial to a project's success. Designers need to address any number of issues in order to ensure that the materials are satisfactory. Generally, they need to consider the following aspects of development when working on materials production:

- ◆ *Cost:* Designers must be sure they know what products are going to cost and that they stay on budget.
- ◆ *Deadlines:* They must set firm deadlines for production of materials and require that vendors stick to the deadlines.
- ◆ *Written agreements:* They must have everything in writing concerning paper, color, size, quantity, fonts, and other variables in their materials.
- ◆ *Samples:* They must always check a sample of the materials before the production begins.
- ◆ *Final approval:* They must be sure to approve final copy of materials, not taking anyone's word for anything.
- ◆ *Pilot-test:* Before producing the final materials, they must conduct pilot tests or have a review by stakeholders in the process, or do both. A pilot test evaluates the entire design, not just materials.

Pilot Testing

Pilot testing is a chance to evaluate a project before it goes into full implementation and is a key component of the development stage. The theory for instructional design is the same as that for a play: Both need rehearsals. It takes time to get all the bugs out of the implementation materials and lesson plans.

It is logical to pilot-test before designers start producing final materials and begin the process of delivering a course. Some designers include pilot testing in the implementation phase, rather than in development, and that is fine. It is more important to test a project before finalizing deliverables than it is to worry about whether testing happens in the development or implementation phases.

Organizations often view a pilot test, or preimplementation practice session, as a luxury. Even if it is a luxury, that doesn't mean designers cannot expose their project to some scrutiny before moving it into implementation. At the very least, it can be useful to do a dry run with a colleague or a friend. Here are some things that designers should look for in a pilot test. If they detect any problems, they should correct them before finalizing that aspect of the program.

- ◆ Does the lesson plan work?
- ◆ Are the directions to the facilitator clear and concise?
- ◆ Are the facilitator's materials appropriate and thorough enough?
- ◆ Are the learner's materials appropriate and thorough enough?
- ◆ Are the support materials (slides, overheads, handouts, and the like) what you expected?
- ◆ Does the timing of each of the segments match your estimates?
- ◆ Are the technology components (audio, video, computers, and so forth) appropriate?
- ◆ Do the instructional methods work as planned?
- ◆ What does not work the way you thought it should?
- ◆ What needs to be changed?

During the review, designers should look for anything that doesn't seem to fit. Sometimes designers' instincts bring to their attention problems that may not be obvious to the SMEs or the client. It is this sixth sense about design that makes the role of the instructional designer so important.

Train-the-Trainer Courses

Another way to discover any problems is with a train-the-trainer (TTT) program, an often-neglected aspect of instructional design. Like analysis, the process of providing this level of support for facilitators involves work and requires resources; in the end, however, the extra effort can make the difference between success and failure.

This critically important aspect of course implementation is often ignored for a variety of seemingly logical reasons. You've probably heard that TTT courses are not necessary because professional facilitators can take any course and implement it with a little practice. Another excuse is that there isn't any time or resources available to bring everyone together for the TTT process. A perennial favorite is the notion that any well-designed course (and all ISD courses are well designed, aren't they?) should not require any additional support for implementation.

As with every aspect of instructional design, the decision to require a TTT course is related to the rest of your course elements. If your system demands it, then you have to consider the ramifications of ignoring the warning. Here's a list of reasons for including a TTT element in instructional design:

◆ new or unfamiliar content
◆ new or unfamiliar delivery system
◆ facilitator population with little or no previous facilitator experience
◆ changes in content specifics that must be taught to facilitators first
◆ new or unfamiliar technology demands on facilitators
◆ online course management systems training specific to content
◆ requirement that content be rigidly and uniformly implemented
◆ licensure or certification required for facilitators.

A TTT course also provides the opportunity for pilot testing of a course, with the caution that the target population may not be in perfect sync with the design plan population profile. In some ways, it may be a preferred method of piloting if the content must also be delivered to the facilitators. This is sometimes the case with mandated training or organization-wide rollouts. In this option, the training is often presented by the instructional design team, SMEs, or some combination of the two.

Train-the-Trainer Course Design

Several styles of TTT courses have evolved over the years, with most being some variation of the "See One, Teach One" model. With this approach, facilitators first observe or participate as learners, one implementation cycle of the course. They then facilitate all or some of the course content while being coached by both the design team and other facilitators. This approach works both in online and in-class settings.

There are many advantages to incorporating a complete observation cycle of the course in this model targeted toward future facilitators. One benefit is that any questions facilitators have about the content can be addressed at the same time as issues associated with their implementation of the content.

The disadvantage of this approach is the time it takes to work through the process. In most cases, it takes at least twice as long to implement the TTT course as the course actually takes in implementation to the intended population profile. That is why variations on this theme are becoming more focused on the unique aspects of a course and less on the actual art of facilitation, except in populations of novice facilitators.

Things to Consider in TTT Designs

As you work through the design of your TTT course, consider the following issues:

- To what degree does the population of facilitators require a facilitation skills upgrade or refresher?
- To what degree is the content new to the facilitators?
- Do you have any doubts about the ability of the facilitators to implement the course in areas that you can address in a TTT session?
- Are there any unique aspects of the course design or implementation that require facilitator participation in the content preparation (for example, field inclusion of data that the facilitator must gather and interpret)?

No matter what you decide about whether to offer a TTT option, at least work through the advantages and disadvantages of your choice. As with most things in ISD, there is no one right or wrong answer.

In Conclusion

Within ISD, the development element is the time when all of the design elements become tangible products and pilot testing takes place. To use the analogy of building a house, the development process sees the blueprint become a tangible, visible building. It is also the time the new house is inspected (pilot testing) and is prepared for occupancy (implementation). For an instructional designer, this is a very busy time with constant quality checks and modifications to plans drawn up in the design phase. This is also the time for any train-the-trainer sessions and final last minute updates to content and materials before implementation.

Discussion Questions

1. As an instructional designer, what should you look for as you evaluate your course in the development phase of ISD?
2. Pilot testing is a key component of the development process. Why do you think it is important to evaluate a course before implementation? What should you look for?
3. As a designer, is it better to hold a train-the-trainer program for a course or just raise the facilitator prerequisites to ensure that the course is implemented to your standards?

Chapter 7

Implementation

Chapter Objectives

At the conclusion of this chapter, you should be able to

- ◆ explain the implementation phase of the ISD process
- ◆ explain Donald Kirkpatrick's level 1 and level 2 evaluation
- ◆ review the evaluation tasks associated with implementation.

---

mplementation is the ISD element that most non-designers consider training and education. It is the time when learners sit in the classroom or in front of a computer for an online course. This phase connects the provider with the end user of the instruction; it is the most recognizable element of the ISD process.

It is an axiom in project management that you are never more than 90 percent complete on any job you are working on. It is the same with instructional design projects. It is time to move on to implementation if a designer has the basics covered, the pilot testing has gone well, and the designer has made the changes. Waiting for that next 10 percent improvement might take longer than the total time allocated for the project.

Not every designer implements the curricula he or she designs. In some cases, a designer may never actually teach the course or be part of a learning technology solution. Designers who do not teach are not necessarily following a faulty line of reasoning. In fact, it is probably a good idea for designers not to teach. Designers who are also facilitators have a tendency to believe they can improvise a fix for missing or faulty design elements on the spot. This is usually not the case. The ability to make alterations on the fly is normally the domain of the designer. Facilitators are not always as experienced or capable of making a faulty lesson plan work as designers might want them to be. Nothing should be left to chance, especially if it allows a design to suffer in the hands of an inexperienced facilitator.

The evaluation of the implementation process must include an evaluation of learners' impressions of the training (that is, Donald Kirkpatrick's level 1) and the validation of objectives being met by learners (that is, Kirkpatrick's level 2).

Kirkpatrick's Levels of Evaluation

Donald Kirkpatrick (1998) has broken evaluation into four levels that are easy to understand. Each of these has specific qualities and fits distinctive needs. Although these levels are linear, designers do not have to use them in any specific order to achieve their evaluation objectives. The four levels of evaluation are as follows:

- ◆ Level 1: Reaction
- ◆ Level 2: Learning
- ◆ Level 3: Behavior
- ◆ Level 4: Results

This chapter includes descriptions of levels 1 and 2, which are essential ingredients of evaluation during implementation. Descriptions of levels 3 and 4 appear in chapter 8, which covers the evaluation phase of ADDIE.

Level 1: Reaction

Anyone who has ever completed an evaluation that asked for a reaction to a training course probably was responding to a level 1 evaluation. The most common evaluations at this level are smile sheets, which ask about likes and dislikes. Smile sheets are so common that some people use the term to refer to all evaluations at this level. Other level 1 evaluations are focus groups that are held after training and selective interviews in which people ask a sample of learners their opinions of training as they leave a program.

The aim of each of these level 1 evaluations is to discover learners' reactions to the process. More than anything, level 1 evaluation provides instant quality control data. ASTD reports that between 72 and 89 percent of organizations use level 1 evaluation (Bassi & Van Buren, 1999).

A good strategy for level 1 evaluation is to determine learners' initial responses to the experience as they exit the training. The freshest and most accurate data for a level 1 evaluation comes at the immediate conclusion of the training. Every minute that elapses from the end of the training to the reaction from a participant adds to the risk that inaccurate data will be collected. After all, designers are looking for a reaction.

Typical questions include:

◆ Was your time well spent in this training?
◆ Would you recommend this course to a co-worker?
◆ What did you like best?
◆ What did you like least?
◆ Were the objectives made clear to you?
◆ Do you feel you were able to meet the objectives?
◆ Did you like the way the course was presented?
◆ Was the room comfortable?
◆ Is there anything you would like to tell us about the experience?

Level 2: Learning

For instructional designers, evaluations at the learning level are tied directly to objectives. These are the evaluation tasks that designers develop to match their objectives. Surprisingly, only 29 to 32 percent of organizations use a level 2 evaluation of behavior (Bassi & Van Buren, 1999). This statistic indicates that less than a quarter of all training is evaluated in relationship to objectives, assuming there are any.

Other Elements of Evaluation

During implementation, other elements of evaluation that must be present are as follows:

◆ evaluation from the perspective of the facilitator
◆ evaluation of the materials or technology
◆ evaluation of the environment (room size, arrangement)
◆ continuity and conformity of implementation with the design plan.

These elements are independent of the Kirkpatrick levels and have the potential for providing data that suggest changes are necessary. Every aspect of the design is subject to further alteration once implemented. As noted earlier, designers should never consider a project more than 90 percent complete. This means they have a work in progress, not a project that has no hope of redemption. Careful evaluation will provide ample opportunities for tweaking during and after implementation.

Even perfectionists can relax, knowing that everything is a work in progress, including content and materials. They may get the check in the mail for their work or be assigned to another project, but the designs they have worked on are still maturing.

In Conclusion

This chapter describes the implementation phase, when participants encounter the instruction, and the importance of evaluation during this period. It discusses levels 1 and 2 of Kirkpatrick's levels of evaluation, which provide designers with information on participants' reactions to the training and on how well the learning meets the objectives.

Discussion Questions

1. Evaluation is a vital element in the implementation phase of ISD. Why do you think that a majority of education and training courses are never reviewed in a way that allows for improvement of the course?
2. Do you feel that level 1 evaluations (reaction) are an important aspect of course implementation?

Chapter 8

Evaluation

At the conclusion of this chapter, you should be able to

- ◆ describe evaluation techniques for all five elements of the ADDIE model
- ◆ list the four levels of evaluation as described by Kirkpatrick
- ◆ design evaluation instruments for all four levels of evaluation.

Evaluating More Than Just Results

Evaluation is more than just a postcourse event. Evaluation takes place in every element of the ADDIE model. Designers even need to evaluate the evaluation process. This multi-dimensional approach to evaluation reflects ISD's systems approach to instructional design. Not only are the traditional evaluations (reflected in learner performance and content mastery) part of the design process, the ISD process itself is reviewed for conformance to best practices throughout the ADDIE elements.

Evaluation of the design process is just as important as a review of the content, and it is an essential part of a design strategy. If the same course receives positive content evaluations but negative process evaluations, there are probably design process problems with either the delivery system or the instructional methods and materials. Positive process evaluations but negative content evaluations from the same course point to such content problems as difficulty of objectives, performance agreement, or other areas related to the subject matter.

Evaluations during each of the other four ADDIE elements provide the quality control mechanism that ensures an honest and meaningful snapshot of both process and product. It is almost impossible for a project to be completed successfully without a comprehensive evaluation strategy that goes beyond looking at the issues associated with learners and facilitators; the process itself must be examined. Analysis, design, development, and implementation all have evaluation needs that designers should include in their projects.

Evaluation in the Analysis Phase

Evaluation in analysis centers on the notion that a project with a solid foundation should never stray too far from where it is designed to be. Even when issues arise that need serious attention, a designer's analysis, if done correctly, will provide the blueprint he or she needs to fine-tune problems later. This is not to say that an analysis stands forever, as an accurate analysis will tell a designer. The evaluation at this point is intended to just make sure that designers have a great starting point.

To incorporate useful evaluation components during ISD, designers need to address certain questions; the responses to these questions will lead designers to the things they'll need to evaluate for the program:

- ◆ Is this an issue or problem that can be completely fixed by training alone?
- ◆ Is this an issue or problem that can be improved by a training intervention?
- ◆ Have you gathered all the data (enough data) concerning:
  - — population
  - — subject matter
  - — organizational goals
  - — learner goals and needs
  - — logistics
  - — resources
  - — constraints?
- ◆ Have you reviewed your analysis results with:
  - — stakeholders
  - — SMEs
  - — target population sample
  - — other designers?

- Have you compared your findings against other internal or external benchmarks?
- Have you double-checked all of the above?

Evaluation in the Design Phase

Design phase evaluation is critical to the success of a project. Designers have little chance for success if they allow a flawed instructional design to move forward to development and implementation. Objectives, evaluation tasks, and all the critical elements of course design take shape in the design phase, and they need to pass some level of evaluation. Evaluations here address problems early and save time and money as an end result.

The value of design phase evaluations is that they enable coordination of information among all those working on a project. For designers working on their own, it is important to have someone review their design phase work because it is easy for designers to lose focus when they become glued to the process. A quick evaluation of both product and process is an absolute necessity.

Information from even the best analysis can go astray in the hands of a technical writer or designer. A SME is the best resource to use to check that the content is correct and clear. A SME's review can prevent embarrassing errors from occurring when the course is rolled out. Designers need to ensure that the following evaluations take place:

- review of all the design plan elements by the SMEs and at least one other designer
- review of all objectives and evaluation tasks by the SMEs and at least one other designer
- review of evaluation strategy and materials
- review of all draft participant materials
- review of all draft facilitator materials
- review of all draft media
- review of everything by the decision makers
- sign-off on everything.

Evaluating Design Elements

The designer must incorporate evaluation components to assess the validity of the objectives and the extent to which the objectives correlate with the desired behavior and the process employed for learning-level (Kirkpatrick level 2) evaluation, that is, performance agreement.

Evaluating Objectives

The first step in evaluating objectives is to identify each component in the objective. Designers should scrutinize the four elements of a learning objective—audience, behavior, condition, and degree—and rate each element from 1 to 10 on the basis of how well it is written. While we will talk in greater detail about objectives in chapter 9 and learn how to rate the elements in chapter 12, knowing that evaluation is required for objectives sets the stage for some of that discussion.

Evaluation in the Development Phase

Evaluation is also important in this phase when many critical decisions are made that can greatly affect the success of your project. Designers must make sure their evaluation plan is ready for the pilot testing of the project. Issues that typically surface during pilot testing are segment timing, deficiencies in materials, lack of clarity in the course structure, and failure to design for the target population. A dozen other minor things may arise as well.

Segment timing is sometimes the hardest task for a designer. Differences in facilitators, equipment, and materials affect timing. A designer should allow for the possibility that any variable may affect timing. It is usually a good design strategy to add extra time. It is also valuable to time several run-throughs of a segment and average the time for the design. It is fairly common to find deficiencies in materials during pilot testing. These problems can range from typographic errors in the copy to offensive graphics or wording. Sometimes simple issues, such as having the materials in the right language, come into play. Just when a designer thinks everything is under control, someone will notice a problem in the materials, perhaps an error in the chief executive officer's name. Designers should fix all errors.

Clarity in the structure of a course is essential if the course is to be effective. Designers do not devote weeks and months to preparing a course just to watch facilitators struggle with the flow of the course or watch participants roll their eyes skyward. Pilot tests often reveal holes in the population analysis, indicating that it undershot or overshot the average learner. It is the designer's responsibility to adjust the population information and content to match the pilot test's findings.

Evaluation in the Implementation Phase

The traditional approach to evaluation during implementation is the use of smile sheets, which show the reaction or response of the learner to the experience. Although these evaluations are an important part of a great evaluation strategy, they are only one small part of what a designer needs to do. Evaluation in this phase needs to cover every aspect of the interaction between the product and the end user.

Table 8.1 shows some components of evaluations during the implementation phase from the perspective of various stakeholders.

Evaluation in the Evaluation Phase

Designers who have evaluated everything in the other four phases will probably find that the evaluation phase is the easiest part of the evaluations. Evaluation products that designers complete during the evaluation phase may include project-end reviews and program evaluations for grants. Each of these is important and requires designers to do some thoughtful retrospection of both process and product for the project.

Project-end reviews have two purposes. First, they look at how well the process worked for delivering the project. Designers should conduct these reviews whether they are working alone or have 30 staff members. To arrive at some objective data, it is important that each person involved reflect on what happened and share those observations with the other people involved.

If the training was contentious, it is best for the people involved to gather the initial feedback anonymously because participants may not want to give honest evaluations if they fear reprisals for their answers. Later, the designer can bring everyone together and work through the problems. If the problems are not fixed at the evaluation stage, they are doomed to be repeated.

Grants usually require program evaluations because the groups that give money want to know what they got for it. These evaluations give designers an opportunity to highlight the best part of the project.

Evaluation data, when presented with graphs or other visual elements, make the case for success. Designers should review the objectives and course rationale and then ensure that the evaluation underscores the results that support those goals.

Table 8.1. Components of Evaluations

Learner	Facilitator	Client	Instructional Designer
Reaction	Reaction	Reaction	Objectives
Accomplishment	Usefulness	Value	Performance
Valuing	Content	Effectiveness	agreement
Investment	Presentation		Content
Reality	Process		Quality
	Reality		Timing
			Participants, clients, and facilitators
			Reality

Kirkpatrick's Levels of Evaluation

This book has made clear the importance of including evaluation through all stages of design and implementation of training. Chapter 7 explained the first two levels of Kirkpatrick's four levels of evaluation. Level 1 is reaction, during which participants tell what they liked and disliked about the training program; and level 2 is learning, during which designers assess whether participants met the objectives. Levels 3 and 4, behavior and results, take place following training. Explanations of levels 3 and 4 follow.

Level 3: Behavior

Post-training evaluation is a level 3 evaluation. The most important question it seeks to answer is, Did the training stick? How much of the training transferred from delivery to the workplace? Between 11 and 12 percent of training is evaluated for behavioral change (Bassi & Van Buren, 1999). This statistic means that only one training project out of 10 is evaluated for effectiveness.

There are a number of ways to conduct level 3 evaluations so that any designer can add this level to a tool kit. Surveys and observation are two powerful ways to evaluate at this level. The thing to remember about this level of evaluation is the behavior. Did the behavior move to the workplace? If designers' objectives are written well, they have half of what they need. The other half is to select a way to measure where participants start and where they are when designers measure long-term results.

Designers who are interested in seeing if participants can meet the training objectives will evaluate learning, whereas those who are interested in seeing if performance has improved will measure behavior. Both of these can be satisfied with evaluation.

For example, evaluations would differ for a course on the use of new software for entering orders in a retail sales environment. A designer is interested in finding out if the course had any impact. Accurate data is available on how long it took to complete a transaction before the training with both the new and old software. At regular intervals, the designer accumulates new data on how long it takes to complete a transaction and compares the numbers. The designer can easily see any difference in time to see if the training had any effect and how much.

Designers who want to find out how much of the training objectives learners can still meet can sample a representative number of participants using the formal evaluation task used during the course. They then compare the scores on an individual or group basis and do the math. This method will go a long way toward evaluating if the content, as well as the instructional and delivery methods, were the best choices for the project.

In situations in which the evaluation is not so simple (with soft skills or affective domain courses, for example), designers can interview or survey participants and gauge the participants' opinion of their ability to still meet the objectives. If possible, designers can also retest a sampling of the participants.

There are three basic reasons why participants may lose the ability to meet objectives after the course, each of which tells the designer something important about the course. The reasons are covered in detail here.

Participants Never Learned the Skill or Concept.

If participants never learned the content, the designer may have a breakdown in the level 3 evaluation of the course objectives. Having a large number of participants in this category usually indicates errors in implementation or design. Designers must carefully evaluate the course design and pay special attention to the population information.

It is possible that the facilitators who carried out the implementation may have done a poor job or didn't follow the lesson plan as provided. It might be that the participants ignored the prerequisites for the program. It is also possible that the evaluation tasks were either ignored or compromised to the point that participants were never evaluated at all. The lack of an evaluation sets up a scenario in which neither participant nor facilitator can really tell if the objectives are being met.

Design flaws could be as simple as poor performance agreement or disregard for a lesson plan structure that supports acquisition of content. Motivation and attitude are also concerns when objectives are not being met across the sample participant pool.

The Skill or Concept Was Never Retained.

Problems with retention may come from any number of issues. The most common problems are too much content in too short a time or a lack of any supportive materials or methods after the conclusion of the course. It is also possible that the content had no meaning or importance to the participant. Ownership of the content is important if participants are to retain information for any length of time. Ownership necessarily implies content and course design that allows that to happen.

The Skill or Concept Was Never Used After the Course.

Designers who determine that participants had no opportunity to use the skills or concepts sometimes face issues beyond their control. They may train 300 women and men to be motorcycle mechanics, but if nearly all of them end up in sales, the training will not stick. These kinds of issues are especially important in psychomotor and cognitive objective domains. Yes, people may be able to ride a bike after many years of no practice, but how many years of practice have they had to support those skills?

Level 4: Results

A level 4 evaluation is about results—bottom-line results. What was accomplished? Did the training pay off? Were the expected or promised results accomplished? This level of evaluation has also drawn more than a few skeptics because inflated claims of return-on-investment (ROI) have sometimes entered into the process and driven many to question any claimed results.

Probably less than three percent of training is evaluated for results (Bassi & Van Buren, 1999). Make no mistake about it: Figuring results can be a tricky and sometimes expensive undertaking. One reason for this is that the value of results can be both monetary and societal in nature. Although the effect on an organization can be calculated with some degree of certainty, the effect on a community is tough to measure and is largely subjective in nature.

However, no one should discount the power that training can have for change in a community. The poison prevention course, for example, is community based, and the impact could be literally lifesaving, a true level 4 result.

In Conclusion

This chapter completes the description of the five elements of the ADDIE model. The final element, evaluation, must be an integral part of all the other elements. This chapter also concludes the description of Kirkpatrick's four levels of evaluation.

Discussion Questions

1. How would you evaluate the evaluation process used during the five elements of the ISD process?
2. Is there ever a case where you think a formal evaluation is not necessary?
3. Do you think the evaluation of the evaluation phase is unnecessary in most situations?
4. Which of Kirkpatrick's four levels of evaluation is the most important in day-to-day ISD work?

◆ Section III

Objectives

Chapter 9

Mastering Objectives

Chapter Objectives

At the conclusion of this chapter, you should be able to

◆ name the four classifications of objectives

◆ differentiate among draft, process, terminal, and enabling objectives

◆ write at least one example of draft, process, terminal, and enabling objectives

◆ describe the four different objective domains

◆ define the performance agreement principle.

The Importance of Mastering Objectives

In every professional endeavor, there are milestones that differentiate the seasoned professional from the rest of the pack. In academics, some consider obtaining a PhD a milestone of differentiation. In many organizations, earning a promotion denotes achievement. For athletes, it might be winning a division or league championship. In the practice of ISD, the milestone of record is the ability to construct and write objectives.

It is a skill that is instantly recognizable by those with the same level of mastery, and it is often a critical criteria for making decisions concerning hiring and promotion within training departments. Writing sound objectives requires detailed knowledge of the process and elements and considerable practice. Telltale signs of designers lacking the necessary skills in writing objectives include the use of non-defined behaviors like "understand" and "learn," writing objectives from the prospective of a teacher, and failing to include condition and degree elements in an objective.

If it is any consolation to those just starting in the field, even seasoned pros in ISD sometimes struggle with writing objectives once they have mastered the basics of the A-B-C-D framework. There are some very important reasons for this phenomenon, the most common being that objectives often serve as the barometer of the weather within a design project. If a designer is struggling to write or perfect objectives for a particular project, there is almost always something else at play causing the problem. A falling project barometer might point toward some less than obvious faults in the design.

First, objectives seldom work when the design project isn't really training or education. It is impossible to write objectives for a seminar or presentation that doesn't include any meaningful student participation or evaluation of mastery. Review your experiences with conference break-out sessions for examples.

Second, in academic settings if there is not evaluation of the mastery of the content by the student, there is no way to write an objective that works within the framework of ISD. Having students sit through a lecture or presentation for the entire implementation time and then evaluating them at the end of the term is not something that rises to the level of acceptable instructional design, and there are no objectives that fit this scenario that are acceptable.

Third, trying to write objectives for a population that is not well defined or is too diverse for the content is a nightmare and signals a designer to return to the analysis and perhaps redefine the population to more closely fit the content. This often happens when a project attempts to combine populations with very diverse levels of content knowledge or interests.

Objectives Basics

In the most basic of terms, objectives define a learner who has reached mastery of a skill or concept related to instruction. Using the building blocks of audience, behavior, condition, and degree, instructional designers provide a framework for constructing units of instruction. In many ways, writing objectives is similar to using a GPS to guide travel. A GPS gathers data like current location, destination, options for routes, and speed and then provides a road map for a trip. Objectives combine current content mastery, final outcomes, evaluation techniques, and options for delivery systems and then provide a road map for instruction. An error in any of the input data puts the final outcome in jeopardy with either a GPS or writing objectives.

Formal and Informal Objectives

For our purposes there are two types of objectives: formal behavioral objectives and informal process-oriented objectives. Ninety percent of your time as a designer will be spent writing formal objectives; however, you may find utility in using informal objectives as you work through a design project.

Legacy approaches to writing objectives focus primarily on formal behavioral objectives, and you will find incredibly detailed coverage of both terminal and enabling objectives in this chapter. In addition, you will learn and practice two new classifications of informal objectives that assist instructional designers with the design process itself. Draft and process objectives expand the role of objectives in instructional design and offer designers two more tools to build their skills.

The A-B-C-D Format: Audience, Behavior, Condition, and Degree

The most common protocol for writing terminal and enabling objectives is what is termed the A-B-C-D format. *A* represents audience, *B* represents behavior, *C* represents conditions, and *D* represents degree. You may have experience writing objectives using a different format, and there are variations on this protocol that run from having just a behavioral element to one format that actually uses five elements. While the four-part objective protocol is the most commonly used and recognized among designers, variations exist, and each should be judged on its fit with a particular project and work environment.

Figure 9.1. The A-B-C-D Format Four-Part Objective Protocol

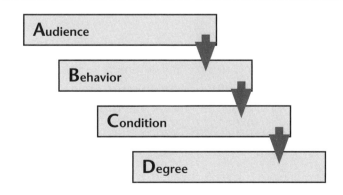

Let's take a more in-depth look at each element; as we do, remember that writing objectives is more than just making sure you have written something for each element. Writing objectives creates the framework for everything else you do in a project. It requires thoughtfulness, investigation, and consideration of all variables before committing to an objective. The journey to writing an objective is in many ways much more important to the design process than the final product that appears in writing. To modify an old cliché: Objectives need to be an inch wide and a mile thick.

Audience

When you think about the end user of a design project, you are thinking about your *audience*. You must be able to capture, in a few words, a very specific design icon for this population. This is much more than just using terms like "learner" and "student" that could easily represent millions of individuals. For pro-level instructional design, you need to be as specific as possible when writing audience statements for your objectives.

At a minimum, designers must make sure that the audience statement is specific to the course and intended population. The crucial element in defining the audience in an objective is the knowledge a designer gathers from such diverse sources as population profiles, SMEs, program and course titles, and project decision makers.

A well-written audience element is a picture of the participants and may include the course or program title, the educational level of the course if it is an academic project, and even the sponsoring organization (if it is an appropriate part of the audience). Several examples are:

- ◆ The New Methods in Marketing participant
- ◆ Handling Stress on the Job student
- ◆ UMBC EDUC 602 student
- ◆ Titanic Limited New Employee Orientation student
- ◆ Local 786 Apprenticeship student
- ◆ Software for Cynics student.

Each of these is more detailed than the common fallback audience statement of student or learner. This reflects both good design practice and an attention to process. As an instructional designer, always spend the time necessary to ensure that your audience statements are based in reality and convey an accurate design interpretation of your audience within the objectives.

Behavior

The most easily recognized element in an objective is the *behavior.* Even poorly written objectives usually contain some form of a behavior statement. In the world of professional instructional design, behaviors are the key focus in the process of designing a course. Audience, condition, and degree elements generally flow naturally from well-written behavior statements in an objective. A close examination of the behavior statement must present a vivid description of an anticipated outcome.

Formatting a behavior statement is important for reasons that include clarity, legality, and consistency. Your choice of wording will have an effect on the design intent of an objective. Most behavior statements are worded in the format "should be able to _____" or "will be able to _____." Designers must be careful about which of these formats they choose for writing their objectives. "Will" and "should" have two distinctly different meanings, and the selection is more than just stylistic.

In some cases where eventual licensure or formal examination is an integral part of a course design, it is not unusual for the wording to read "must be able to_____" or "is required to_____" since the standard applies to more than just an objective. Anything less and the standard has no meaning in the context of the required licensure. This is especially true with medical professionals such as paramedics and EMTs who are required to renew their credentials on a regular basis and anything less than 100 percent mastery is usually unacceptable.

Promising that a learner "will" be able to do something has its own set of concerns. It is much different than stating one "should" be able to do something when writing objectives. The argument against "will" is based on the concept of promising absolute results. For example, if an objective states that "the Golfing for Beginners participant *will* be able to score in the low 60s for 18 holes of golf," the designer had better have one great golf program developed! *Designers should not make promises they cannot keep.*

The behavior statement must not use verbs such as "learn" and "understand" because there is no way to measure or observe them. Just because a learner's frequent nods and thoughtful looks give the facilitator reason to believe the participant is learning and understanding does not make it true. Behavior needs to be observable and measurable. Verbs such as "create," "write," "list," "construct," and "repair" are observable, measurable, and suitable for statements of behavior in written objectives. Table 9.1 offers more examples of verbs that work well in behavior statements.

Table 9.1. Observable and Measurable Verbs

Apply	Employ	Rank
Argue	Estimate	Rearrange
Assess	Examine	Recognize
Calculate	Explain	Record
Change	Express	Relate
Choose	Extrapolate	Repeat
Cite	Formulate	Rephrase
Classify	Identify	Report
Combine	Illustrate	Restate
Compare	Infer	Schedule
Conclude	Integrate	Score
Contrast	Interpolate	Sketch
Criticize	Interpret	Solve
Decide	Inventory	Specify
Define	Judge	Standardize
Derive	Manage	Tell
Design	Measure	Translate
Diagram	Name	Transmit
Differentiate	Operate	Underline
Discuss	Organize	Use
Dramatize	Prescribe	Validate
Draw up a list	Question	

Make sure that the behavior matches both the objective domain (as discussed later in this chapter) and the expected mastery. This is where performance agreement issues can arise and being able to avoid them with excellent objectives is the best way to avoid any problems with the relationship between objectives and evaluation tasks.

Condition

The *condition* statement in an objective provides two important design elements: the context of the learning environment and the framework for evaluation for each learning event. Generally, condition statements begin with the word "given" followed by the elements that relate to the objective. For example:

◆ given classroom discussion, handouts, and a short presentation
◆ given a working computer, access to the Internet, browser software, and a study guide
◆ given a chapter reading in the text, participation in a role play, and facilitation

- ◆ given a real-life scenario, a resuscitating dummy, and a portable defibrillator
- ◆ given a model 19t54x digital multi-meter and a malfunctioning 15 amp breaker.

Conditions may include tangible things, like tools, books, equipment, or hardware; they may also have their basis in an instructional method. For example, a condition might read, "given a screwdriver and 10 screws" or "provided with a 1329A test set." Other less tangible conditions are "following participation in a role play" or "after having read chapter 4 of the text."

Although it may appear at times that condition statements are either too obvious to be useful or overly complicated, subtle differences in context can sink an otherwise great course. Some facilitators omit books or other reading material, or instructional methods intended for the course are replaced or eliminated based on a facilitator's whim. Failing to mention a specific book, other reading material, or an instructional method might seem insignificant, but it could result in a facilitator's taking a different approach to teaching. General condition statements, such as "when completed with this course," are inadequate because they do not provide any foundation from which to work. Try to be as thorough as possible in setting the context.

In a poison prevention course, for example, the conditions might be the following:

- ◆ given a planning sheet and sketch of a home or office
- ◆ given a practice session with another participant in the course
- ◆ given several real-life scenarios of potential poisoning hazards.

Each of these conditions provides a context that supports the other elements of an objective.

Degree

The *degree* element in an objective is the evaluative finishing line of mastery. In colloquial terms, an objective's behavior element says "jump" and the degree element tells the learner "how high." Degrees are the real anchor for evaluation, and once a standard for mastery is established, it is very easy to design a course based on these standards.

As you consider an objective's degree element, you may want to use the mastery continuum principle to make decisions about level of difficulty based on your population and relative content experience. Populations with little previous content experience or learners who should be able to meet mastery with more than one attempt might best be served with degree statements like these:

- ◆ at least once without error within three attempts
- ◆ until completed without error
- ◆ three or more times
- ◆ at least five times during a practice session.

For populations that are near the expert level with a specific content, degree statements like this might be more appropriate:

- ◆ without error
- ◆ on three different models of the equipment
- ◆ within 5 minutes
- ◆ a grade of 90 percent or better on a qualifying exam.

If your objective is in the affective domain, a different perspective on degree statements is sometimes necessary since binary evaluations are less important than measures of participation, for example:

- ◆ by offering an opinion
- ◆ citing an example
- ◆ participating in a discussion
- ◆ completing a personal skills inventory.

All of these degree statements meet the criterion of being a good objective element because they are observable and measurable. No doubt should exist in anyone's mind about what needs to be done to meet the objective.

Instructional designers should not write degree statements that include ambiguous words. Using "safely," "carefully," "honestly," and similar adverbs only creates confusion in evaluation since every learner could have a different interpretation of what any of these mean. If you insist on using them, they require additional clarifying information if they are put in an objective. The word "safely," for example, would not be measurable in the phrase "use the machine safely," but would be measurable used this way: "will be performed safely, as documented in the Occupational Safety and Health Administration (OSHA) 500 standards." Other degree statements that are generally not acceptable include these:

- ◆ at the discretion of the instructor
- ◆ after participating
- ◆ until finished
- ◆ at the end of the course
- ◆ until tired.

It is also necessary to use percentages carefully in degree statements. A passing grade of 85 percent or better on the final exam is fine as a degree; however, a cardiopulmonary resuscitation (CPR) class that says students will be able to perform CPR correctly 85 percent of the time would not be an acceptable threshold. For certain skill sets, anything less than 100 percent proficiency is of dubious value or wholly unacceptable.

Percentages must be reasonable. It is better to have an employee of a coffee shop meet an objective of making four acceptable lattes in a row, rather than one of operating the latte machine correctly at least 70 percent of the time.

Terminal and Enabling Objectives

When most designers talk about objectives they are referring to behavioral objectives, and generally these are divided into two classifications: terminal objectives and enabling objectives. Terminal objectives should be viewed as the final or exit competency expected of a learner. Enabling objectives *enable* a terminal objective by providing a detailed set of objectives that break down a terminal objective to its most basic learning elements (see figure 9.2).

Terminal Objectives

As the name suggests, *terminal objectives* define terminal or exit competencies expected of a learner at the end of a course, module, or program. These are meant to express the sum of the objectives written for a course. If you are designing a course with the content area of learning to ride a bike, a terminal objective for this course might read like this: Given a functioning two-wheeled bike, the Learning to Bike Basics student should be able to ride a bike for 100 feet or more without assistance (see figure 9.3).

Figure 9.2. Terminal and Enabling Objectives

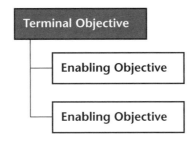

Figure 9.3. Example of Terminal Objective

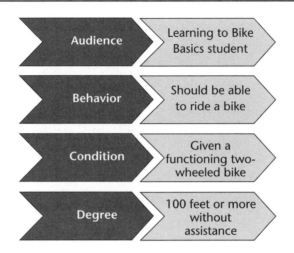

Audience	Learning to Bike Basics student
Behavior	Should be able to ride a bike
Condition	Given a functioning two-wheeled bike
Degree	100 feet or more without assistance

A more detailed terminal objective is shown in this example for a course on the safe handling of asbestos on a job site:

◆ Given a realistic scenario depicting the handling and disposal of asbestos at a work site, the participant in the asbestos supervisor's course should be able to supervise the work of at least two asbestos removal technicians. The participant must comply with all OSHA standards that relate to the specific situation depicted in the scenario. No deficiency will be allowed, and the participant must repeat the process until able to comply with the zero-deficiency standard.

This description clearly states the skill the participant should have at the end of the course. There can be as many terminal objectives as needed, whether one or a thousand. In large projects, instructional designers can end up with design plans that fit in a series of three-ring binders, but it is also possible to have just one. The number varies with the design needs.

Enabling Objectives

On the other hand, *enabling objectives* are the supporting behaviors that, when grouped together, build the path to a terminal objective. Using our bicycling example, we might see several enabling objectives that read like this:

◆ Given a functioning two-wheeled bike with training wheels, the Learning to Bike Basics student should be able to adjust the handlebars to the correct height in two attempts.

◆ Given a functioning two-wheeled bike with training wheels, the Learning to Bike Basics student should be able to adjust the seat height so that each leg is almost fully extended during the down stroke on the peddles.

But as you can see, each enabling objective supports and adds detail to the terminal objective's outcome of being able to ride the bike without assistance. There could easily be ten or more enabling objectives in our example that support our one terminal objective.

In our asbestos training course example, the learner will have to display mastery of all the tasks that will be taught. Following are two possible enabling objectives for the asbestos course:

◆ Given a hammer and chisel and while suited, the technician should be able to remove sprayed asbestos from a wall or ceiling without being exposed to the asbestos dust.

◆ Given a bag of asbestos materials collected on the work site, the technician should be able to dispose of the material in the removal containers without any leakage of material.

Enabling objectives are always sequenced to allow for a gradual building of skills from simple to complex. You will learn more about this in chapter 15, "The Content Mastery Continuum and the Mastery Tipping Point."

Objectives Dos and Don'ts

Behavioral objectives should always be written in the A-B-C-D format. The one exception to this rule is for enabling objectives, which don't always require an audience statement. In all cases, terminal and enabling objectives must provide a formal, well-written framework that allows design projects to grow and mature.

Designers frame objectives from the perspective of the end user of the training, not the facilitator. They do not say what a facilitator is supposed to do, but what the learner should be able to do at the end of the course. It would not be correct to say, "The facilitator will teach the students how to use the fax machine" or "At the end of this course, the facilitator will have presented all of the course materials in a friendly and persuasive manner." Learners are the focus of objectives because they are the reason for the course. Although directions to a facilitator are important to instructional design, they say nothing about what the leaner is supposed to do at the end of the course.

Objectives are always written for the individual learner. Writing an objective that describes more than one learner presents a number of design issues, the least of which is how designers provide any meaningful evaluation. It is also problematic for a designer to think of an entire subset of learners as if they were a single learner. To do so challenges clarity. An objective for a group project can be written at the level of the single learner.

Following is an objective for a group:

◆ Given paint, brushes, and a bare wall, the apprentices in the Painting for Pleasure course will create a mural with the dimensions of at least 4 feet by 4 feet.

Better is this group objective:

◆ Given paint, brushes, and a bare wall, an apprentice in the Painting for Pleasure course will create a mural element with other apprentices, each of whom contributes at least one section of the completed work.

The second objective makes it possible for each learner to be evaluated on his or her individual accomplishment, without relying on other learners. Following is a learner-centered version of an objective on use of a fax machine:

◆ Given a working fax machine, the Office Technology participant should be able to send a two-page fax to another location without error.

Objectives are necessary for each learning activity. Every concept, skill, or objective-worthy behavior needs to be identified and honored with an objective. If an activity is important enough to be included in a design plan, then it is important enough to have a written objective. An objective is the best way to guarantee that the designer will be able to evaluate whether course participants have mastered each skill or concept for which there is instruction. Designers have a tendency to write either too many or too few objectives. They can decide if they need to write an objective by answering the question, "Does it stand on its own?"

Objectives Are Not Goals

Goals and objectives are not the same things. *Goals* are general statements of desired outcomes, whereas *objectives* are detailed statements of outcomes. Draft and process objectives are a much closer fit for expressing these interests. For example, a process objective might be to improve communications within an organization, whereas an enabling or terminal objective for that design need might be:

◆ Given several role-play situations and class discussions, the Better Communications participant should be able to develop at least three specific ways to improve intraoffice communications.

Designers should write objectives so that they can be met within the implementation time of the course. This is a nice way of saying, "Don't promise something you have no control over." Setting an objective that states that a learner "should be able to construct an effective marketing plan" is much different from an objective that promises "increased sales in 6 months." Designers only have control over the process of training a learner to assemble a marketing plan; they cannot influence sales volume.

What Objectives Should Be

Objectives should be measurable and observable. An objective that cannot be measured or observed is probably not going to have much chance for evaluation. That shortcoming significantly diminishes the usefulness of the objective.

Several different methods are available for writing objectives. The most recognized format contains the elements of the previously mentioned A-B-C-D format (audience, behavior, condition, and degree). Some other formats require a fifth element, whereas still others require only three. The adding and subtracting of elements is usually the result of adding more detail to a behavior or eliminating the audience element.

How instructional designers write and format their objectives is up to them. Sometimes it is a good practice to combine elements of a terminal objective with those of an enabling objective to provide a much more readable format, as in the following example:

◆ Given all required tools and safety equipment, the participant in the asbestos supervisor course should be able to:
  — remove asbestos, without exposure, wearing proper safety equipment
  — remove debris from the work site using the proper containers without any leakage of material.

It is important that all the objectives are in the proper order. In the previous example, the participant must wear the proper equipment before removing debris, so that objective comes first.

Objective Domains

Objective domains are categories or classifications of objectives that assist instructional designers in determining a number of important design elements. The four objective domains are cognitive, affective, psychomotor, and interpersonal (see figure 9.4). Primarily, they assist instructional designers in determining how to structure objectives, evaluations, and delivery systems. Designers seldom mix objectives and evaluation tasks from different objective domains because they may then lack validity.

Figure 9.4. Objective Domains

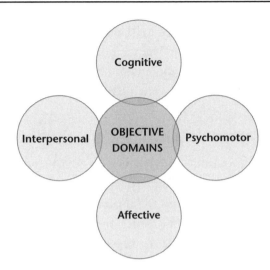

What follows is an example that demonstrates the importance of objective domains to designers without going into the science behind domains. An instructional designer who was working on a training program for technicians to repair a certain type of computer might use all four domains in the following way in the design process:

- *Cognitive domain:* A learner should be able to know how to repair the equipment set.
- *Psychomotor domain:* A learner should be able to physically remove cases and insert boards and should be able to perform other skills requiring the use of the body.
- *Affective domain:* Learners should be able to offer strategies to overcome negative feelings about repairing certain models.
- *Interpersonal domain:* Learners should be able to provide excellent customer service.

Following are descriptions of each domain in detail.

Cognitive Domain

The cognitive domain usually accounts for most of an instructional designer's objectives. Generally, the definition of cognitive domain in training is the cognitive, or thinking, actions of the brain that result from the act of processing sensory information. The cognitive domain can be viewed as the output from a process. One could argue successfully that every objective has some component of the cognitive domain. The distinctions among domains become important because of overlaps like this. The output of the behavior is the point at which instructional designers can judge the predominant domain. For example, if the output from a behavior is mostly the processing of data, then the domain would be cognitive.

Following are examples of objectives in the cognitive domain:

- ◆ The learner should be able to distinguish circuit boards 14R and 17Y.
- ◆ The learner should be able to add and subtract fractions.
- ◆ The learner should be able to identify risk factors associated with hepatitis.
- ◆ The learner should be able to recite the organizational oath.

Psychomotor Domain

The psychomotor domain is undoubtedly the easiest one to identify. If an objective mainly requires movement, it is probably psychomotor. Learning to operate a machine or using a computer mouse are two examples of skills that are in the psychomotor domain. Although they both have some cognitive influence, they require movement for successful completion of the objective. Here are some objectives for psychomotor behaviors:

- ◆ The learner should be able to change the toner cartridge in the copy machine.
- ◆ The learner should be able to assemble circuit pack 2349.
- ◆ The learner should be able to repair a broken antenna on a field radio.
- ◆ The learner should be able to attach option 7T to the main assembly.

Interpersonal Domain

Alex Romiszowski (1981) established the premise for the interpersonal domain in his publication "The How and Why of Performance Objectives." Although most instructional design literature pays far too little attention to this concept, it is a vital fourth dimension to the objective domain concept and, in practice, offers the missing element that defines key objective sets that exist in the real world.

Many of the soft skill training programs in large organizations are in some way related to the interaction of two or more individuals. This is why interpersonal behaviors are important. Designers are often forced into serving as mediators in organizational disputes involving individuals or departments. Dealing with such interpersonal problems requires a separate objective set. Examples of objectives involving interpersonal behaviors include the following:

- ◆ The learner should be able to identify an area of disagreement between the two departments.
- ◆ The learner should be able to answer the phone and take a message without displaying obvious anger or impatience.

- ◆ The learner should be able to participate in a role-play situation reflecting the key areas of conflict in the office.
- ◆ The learner should be able to answer a question without resorting to name-calling.

Affective Domain

Objectives in this domain are soft skills that are difficult to observe and measure. Constructing evaluation tasks for affective domains is difficult and may be the reason that some designers shy away from writing this objective.

Many instructional designers think it is nearly impossible to write a behavior statement for some affective domain objectives. Others argue that you cannot change the way someone "feels" about a subject. It is not easy, but it is usually possible to work effectively as a designer in these behaviors. The designer cannot work to change a learner's attitude, just the learner's behavior. For example, a training program on customer service for new clerks in a retail environment would have affective domain objectives. If the goal of the training is to influence behavior, and not the interpersonal aspects of the issue (that is, how a clerk tells a customer that 32-inch jeans do not fit comfortably around a 48-inch waist), an instructional designer would write objectives for affective domain behaviors.

An affective domain objective for this situation might be stated like this:

- ◆ The learner in the New Clerks Training will describe at least two anger-displacement strategies in a case study situation involving a customer being aggressive about a return with no receipt.

The intent of this behavior statement is to get the new clerk to process the anger and maintain composure in this difficult situation, which the clerk will likely face on the job. It certainly is not the intent of the objective to keep the clerk from wanting to confront the customer.

Affective domain objectives and the issues associated with trying to operationalize the process will always be difficult. It can be very hard to separate behavior from the trigger that brings the response, and that is a challenge designers constantly face. Workplace violence is a good example of an affective domain issue.

A strategy for the training is to address individual worker's violent tendencies, and that involves affective domain. Helping supervisors deal with potentially violent workers before violence erupts addresses the interpersonal domain. Clearly, there are elements of all four domains at work in these examples. However, the focus is on one domain, whereas the others play an enabling role. Following is how an objective might be written for the affective domain in the workplace violence example:

◆ Given a stop-action role-play situation in which the Workplace Violence participant assumes the role of a worker who feels anger at another worker on the job, the participant should be able to successfully articulate at least two strategies to keep his or her anger under control when the role play stops for discussion.

Following is how an objective might be written for the interpersonal domain in the workplace violence example:

◆ Given a role-play situation in which the Workplace Violence Prevention for Supervisors participant assumes the role of a supervisor who is facilitating a potentially violent workplace confrontation, the learner should be able to enact a strategy that prevents the situation from moving from confrontation to violence.

The difference in these two objectives is their focus. One approach intends to work within the emotional framework of the individual, whereas the other relies on interpersonal skills to diffuse a violent situation. Both have the same long-term goal of stopping violence, but they approach it in very different ways.

Using Objective Domains in the Design Process

Once designers establish their primary objective domain, they should think about consistency throughout the design in domain-related areas and consistency with analysis data. Instructional designers must ensure consistency throughout domain-related areas such as performance agreement, materials, instructional methods, evaluation techniques, and any design elements that are influenced by domain. Crossing domains will disrupt the design and confuse or negate the objectives. For example, objectives written for a training program that instructs paramedics in the use of a defibrillator are probably going to be psychomotor. The designer's objectives and course design should stay largely in that domain. If the course ends up focusing on the emotional trauma associated with being a first responder, the designer has switched domains and endangered the original goal of the course, the use of a defibrillator.

To maintain consistency with analysis data, designers should not cross domains when moving from analysis to design. They must not ignore analysis data by misreading the predominant domain. For example, in a course for paramedics, if the analysis data show that learners are worried about learning when and if to use the siren and lights on the ambulance, the topic of the final course should not focus on how to use specific brands and models of sirens and lights. Rather, the topic should be when-and-if concerns about the use of sirens and lights.

Degree of Difficulty

A number of taxonomies suggest that certain behaviors are more difficult to learn than others. For example, predicting is more difficult than defining, and distinguishing is less difficult than synthesizing.

A designer needs to know the *degrees of difficulty* to ensure that an objective follows a continuum from simple to complex or from easy to hard. Most learning theories suggest that moving a learner slowly up the slope of difficulty allows a gradual accumulation of information. People who are learning to play an instrument start with simple exercises to help them learn the basics. As they acquire more skill, they move to playing sequences of notes and then to playing short melodies.

As designers develop their objectives and evaluation tasks, they must keep in mind the degree of difficulty of single objectives and then the sequencing of all the objectives in a project. A good practice is to assign a numerical value for difficulty from 1 to 10 and then to rate each objective. The objectives should begin with the lower numbers and proceed to the higher. By following that sequence, it would be easy for designers to see if they have a problem in their sequencing.

In a course about running a marathon, for example, designers would sequence objectives in such a way that the less difficult skills or concepts are given in the beginning and the more difficult are offered at the end. For example, an early objective might be for a participant to take short, 1-mile runs every other day for a week. This objective is relatively easy compared with a terminal objective of running a 26-mile race and would probably rate a 1 or 2, whereas a series of 5-mile runs would rate a 4 or 5. The terminal objective of running 26 miles would rate the maximum (10) in this series because it is the most difficult objective in the course.

Draft Objectives

Draft objectives are the younger sibling of the formal terminal and enabling behavioral objective statements of what a learner should be able to accomplish at the end of a course, module, or program. Draft objectives are meant to be the bridge between initially identifying concepts and skills within a design and later writing formal objectives. They are an excellent way of working with SMEs and others using nontechnical terms or processes and yet allow a designer to gather the data necessary to drill down to the more technical detail necessary for a design plan.

In comparison to formal objectives, there are two main differences in the way these are written. Draft objectives are not expected to contain audience, condition, or degree statements, or even well-defined behaviors. Additionally, draft objectives are not necessarily grouped or subdivided into terminal and enabling categories.

Draft objectives are written to reflect individual learning episodes and they may or may not be initially grouped with other objectives to build more traditional terminal and enabling status. The process of grouping and categorizing comes after the process of writing draft objectives. Examples of draft objectives for a course in the content area of instructional design might be:

- Define the term *system*.
- List the elements of the ADDIE ISD model.
- Give an example of designer activities in each element of the ADDIE model.
- List the four parts of an objective.
- Define the term *terminal objective*.
- Define the term *enabling objective*.
- Write terminal objectives.
- Write enabling objectives.
- List the elements in a design plan.
- Prepare a draft rationale for a course or program.

An example of grouped draft objectives for the same ISD course in the content area of prerequisites would be:

- Define the term *prerequisite*.
- Define the term *facilitator prerequisite*.
- List examples of facilitator prerequisites.
- Define the term *participant prerequisite*.
- List examples of participant prerequisites.

Process Objectives

Process objectives are general expressions of direction or outcome that do not necessarily reflect specific learner performance or behavior, yet are important considerations for the designer to keep in mind during the design process. Although some process objectives may seem like traditional goals, a process objective provides clear direction to the design process. Goals are general statements whereas process objectives are more concrete, yet they do not contain the level of detail that behavioral objectives do. Once again, process objectives allow for a more efficient connection with non-designers participating in the design process. Examples of process objectives for a project might be:

- Building learner identity with the sponsor is important.
- Case study examples must be written using content derived from actual cases.
- Excellent facilitation skills required for this content.
- Learner motivation issues must be addressed early in this course.

Process objectives are not only one of the building blocks of instructional design, but also are the foundation for building a solid working relationship with clients and other professionals in the design process. In some ways, they are the Rosetta stone of this process; they allow an avenue for translation for the many participants in the process. Everyone's ideas and suggestions have a common language that is operationalized easily by all involved, and the language and operating environment of each participant is translated readily into tangible discussion and action points.

Imagine having a design team that consists of one instructional designer, one client representative, one writer, and one media designer. Depending on the experience of each of these individuals with the design process, you might encounter a range of communications and project style challenges. By starting with a common set of process objectives, a designer will be able to start the project with an informal set of guidelines to work with. Because this preliminary step involves reducing these ideas to writing, you not only have a paper trail, but also have tangible points for discussion if everyone isn't on the same page in the design or project process. This element of the process alone can save a project, as well as many hours or days of frustration and misunderstanding among participants.

Evaluation Tasks and the Performance Agreement Principle

The usefulness of objectives is severely jeopardized without evaluation tasks. In fact, it makes little sense to bother with objectives if there is no intention to evaluate a learner's progress toward meeting them. Designers must develop the ability to construct evaluation tasks. The tasks must not be a hurdle in themselves; they must be achievable and based on real life. Examples of simple evaluation tasks are as follows:

- ◆ Using the circuit pack labeled B-75, replace the defective processor board on the server and confirm that the server is operating without error.
- ◆ You have until 4:00 p.m. to correctly solve all 25 math problems.

Evaluation tasks are created during the design phase to ensure that every objective has a corresponding learner-level evaluation as part of the course. Every objective needs to have this evaluation to ensure performance agreement.

Performance Agreement Principle

Performance agreement is a design term that describes the process of matching objectives and evaluation tasks together in a curriculum (see figure 9.5). This is a key concept in ISD because it mandates that objectives always have an evaluation and that evaluations always have an objective.

One of the reasons that ISD is so useful is that it sticks to a process. The correct use of ISD makes it almost impossible to leave out major chunks of curriculum design. Performance agreement insists that instructional designers pay careful attention to balance in their design work by insisting on an evaluation of every objective.

As an example, here is an objective written for a segment of a course called Sales for the Beginner:

◆ Given a realistic role-play situation with Sales for the Beginner, the learner playing the part of the salesperson should be able to present three reasons why the client should purchase a specific product.

With the objective written, the instructional designer will have to construct an evaluation task. Here is a suggested approach:

◆ You have just entered the office of a major client. You have to make a case for buying your top-line product. It is important that you present at least three reasons why the client should purchase your product.

The designer would then have to measure the performance agreement. The behavior, condition, and degree statements are the key elements the designer would have to match in the objective and the evaluation task. The first step in determining performance agreement is to identify these three elements in each. Table 9.2 shows each element in the objective and the evaluation task. When all the behavior, condition, and degree statements agree, the designer has created a performance agreement.

A good test of objectives is whether instructional designers are able to come up with an evaluation task. If it is not possible, the objective may be flawed in one or all of the three elements.

Figure 9.5. Performance Agreement Principle

Performance Agreement		
All of these match between an objective and an evaluation task.		
Behavior	Condition	Degree

Table 9.2. The Performance Agreement Match

	Objective	Evaluation Task
Behavior	. . . the learner . . . should be able to present . . . reasons why the client should purchase a specific product	. . . you present . . . reasons why the client should purchase your product
Condition	Given a realistic role-play situation with . . . learner playing the part of the salesperson . . .	You have just entered the office of a major client. You have to make a case for buying your top-line product.
Degree	. . . present three reasons . . .	. . . three reasons . . .

Correcting Performance Agreement Problems

The best way to fix problems with performance agreements is to change either the objective or the evaluation task to ensure the two are in agreement. Designers should base their decisions about which to change on their analysis and the context of their course. Consider the following objective:

◆ Provided with a stethoscope and blood pressure measuring equipment, the Nursing 304 student should be able to determine the blood pressure of five patients, as verified by the instructor.

If the evaluation task and objective do not agree, the designer could change the evaluation task to have the student take the blood pressure of all the patients. Another possibility would be to change the objective to include making a determination of need and then measuring the blood pressure of only those patients who need to have it done.

Take a look at the following example:

◆ Given participation in a role-play situation, the Effective Intercultural Communications student should be able to say hello and good-bye in at least two languages other than English.

If the evaluation task and objective do not agree, the designer could change the objective from the requirement for hello and good-bye fluency to something else, or the designer could rewrite the evaluation task to have the student say hello in a large hotel lobby where numerous languages are being spoken.

In Conclusion

This chapter has begun the exploration of design. It covers the process of writing four-part objectives and explains how instructional designers use terminal and enabling objectives and the objective domains to make certain the objectives make sense. It explains how instructional designers adhere to the performance agreement principle to ensure they can assess the objectives.

The next section addresses design and lesson plans, crucial aspects of any instructional design project.

Discussion Questions

1. Describe at least three benefits of using behavioral objectives as an instructional designer.
2. Is it important to differentiate between terminal and enabling objectives when designing a new course?
3. Is recognizing objective domains an important consideration in writing objectives?
4. Should seeking performance agreement in a design be a critical issue?
5. Do you see any value in using draft and process objectives during the design process?

◆ Section IV

Design and Lesson Plans

Chapter 10

Design Plans

Chapter Objectives

At the conclusion of this chapter, you should be able to

◆ describe the elements of a design plan

◆ construct a design plan.

This chapter gives you the opportunity to assemble one of the two major components of quality instructional design—the design plan. The design plan serves as the anchor for the entire instructional design process. Once you have mastered the individual elements of a design plan, you will have the skills necessary to develop one for any project you work on in the future. The poison prevention course provides a model for the discussion in this chapter.

The Design Plan

The process of designing an instructional program goes beyond delivering the training. Although most observers consider implementation the most perceptible part of the process, it just touches the surface of the designer's work. Even a great musician rarely just picks up an instrument and plays a song well the first time. Musicians spend a great deal of time working so that the notes their audience hears come to life. The concept is similar for a design project.

Most learners, and others outside the design process, see only the facilitator and the other learners. They are seldom aware of the hours, days, or months that went into the project from the design perspective. This is where a *design plan* comes into play. Before, during, and after the observable aspects of the training are implemented, the designer's work is documented in a package of design elements that outlines the basics of the project from the ISD perspective.

A design plan is also the detailed explanation that every project should have to be complete. Designers who cannot answer all the questions raised in a design plan may need to spend more time reviewing each element to ensure they have a well-designed project.

A description of each of these elements follows. Designers may come up with other things that are important for their project, and they should add or subtract sections as their projects demand. Nevertheless, it is best to include them all to ensure a complete design plan that covers all the bases. For example, designers in the training or education department of an organization may feel that facilitator prerequisites are unnecessary because the facilitators are known, and so they may leave them out of the design plan. There is no right or wrong when it comes to what is included. The important point is that designers have a design plan and that it covers any elements necessary to explain the project fully.

Rationale

A *rationale* is the mission statement for the project. A designer who can capsulize his or her project into a short, tightly written narrative has several important pieces of information about the effort and can communicate them to others. First, the designer knows where the project is going. Second, the designer knows how to get there. Third, the designer knows why it is important to go there in the first place. The rationale is comparable to a lawyer's opening statement.

A typical rationale is several paragraphs to several pages long. It should not be a word longer than it needs to be or a word shorter than is necessary to make the case for the project. Designers have to make sure they have a mission statement mentality as they write the rationale. In other words, they should make their points as if they were writing a mission statement for the project. Designers should let their cerebral side come to the surface as they compose a rationale for the project. The rationale needs to answer several central questions:

- ◆ What are the reasons for having the course?
- ◆ What population or populations does it serve?
- ◆ Who is sponsoring the course?
- ◆ What is unique about it?
- ◆ Why should anyone participate as a learner or sponsor?

A rationale for the model poison prevention course is worded like this:

Accidental poisonings in the home are a horrifying fact of life in too many families. All it takes to set the scene for this tragedy is for someone to have a short lapse of memory during which the person forgets to close a cabinet door or a container of prescription medication. Those openings can be invitations to a curious child. Accidental poisonings can be easily prevented by implementation of some simple steps. The Poison Prevention in the Home course is designed to provide a quick, powerful lesson in poison prevention for any concerned adult.

Sponsored by a national health-care provider, this course offers a unique method of identifying potential poisoning hazards. Participants draw a map of their residence and highlight the areas that represent poisoning hot spots. Participants make a list of poisons in that location and complete a plan of action for dealing with any hazards. Because poisonings do not always occur in conveniently marked locations around the house, the course employs a secondary strategy for identifying hazards not usually associated with a specific room. Participants then list these hazards and develop a strategy to address those poisons.

This course is implemented in less than 90 minutes, with actual course time set at 60 minutes. The additional 30 minutes are for housekeeping items and a question-and-answer session after the formal class. To allow participant interaction, the anticipated class size is 25 or fewer for each offering.

Handouts, a DVD, and computer-based slides will be provided for each facilitator. A train-the-trainer session will be required for each facilitator before he or she will be certified to implement the course. The target population for this course is adults with an interest in preventing poisoning in their homes.

Target Population

For the design and the learners to resonate together in a project, designers need to define the *target population* or *end user*. The description does not have to be a long narrative, but it should cover all the bases. Although everyone involved in a project should be aware of its target population, people still make surprising assumptions about who will attend their courses. Some of these assumptions may be so irrelevant for the true population of the course that, if not corrected, they could ruin any chance that a design could work. For a course in a technical area, for example, designers once assumed that their audience would include newly hired, entry-level personnel as well as seasoned veteran technicians or supervisors. Unless these designers refined the target population early in the process, they would have wasted valuable resources of time and money either by implementing the course to the wrong population or redesigning it at a point that required making major revisions of content and techniques. To avoid that lose-lose proposition, it is important to focus on the target population section of the design plan.

The target population statement must include those aspects of the population that can cause problems from a design perspective. Too much detail is clutter that should be avoided. It is not necessary to hinge design decisions on population elements such as gender and age if they will not affect course content. Designers should just stick to the facts that illustrate the population and have the potential to cause them problems.

As designers begin to write the target population section of the design plan, they should close their eyes and picture the audience waiting for the course to begin. If they cannot give a detailed description of that group, they have either a design problem to solve or an open-enrollment situation. Designers should picture a group of people slowly emerging from a dense fog and, as they get closer, begin to add details to what they are viewing. Then they should write down what they see and add as much detail as the situation demands. In some instructional designs, the population overview can become complex. Following is a description of the target population of the poison prevention course:

This population is largely adults with a high school education and an interest in preventing accidental poisoning in their homes. This group will be self-motivated to attend based on the marketing strategy employed by the course sponsor.

In practice, target populations are lengthy and include specific data and analysis.

Description

This *description* section of the design plan paints a picture of the structure of the training. Common elements to consider for the course description are:

- ◆ total course length
- ◆ module length (if appropriate)
- ◆ instructional method
- ◆ materials.

For the poison prevention model course, a description looks like this:

The poison prevention training is structured and lasts 60 minutes. Instructional methodologies employed include lecture, small group activities, and learner presentation and discussions. The room must be compliant with the Americans with Disabilities Act (ADA) and have the capacity to provide computer projection. Recommended class size is 25 or fewer unless an assistant is available.

Designers must make sure their course description provides enough detail to depict the design of the project accurately.

Objectives

The foundation and direction of the design plan are set under *objectives*, and everything else builds from them. All the terminal objectives go in this section. At times, the number of objectives may be so large that a designer must list them in an appendix or elsewhere for easy reference. Large projects can easily have hundreds of objectives. The poison prevention course has the following objective:

> *Given handouts, a job aid, and class discussion, the Poison Prevention in the Home participant should be able to create a plan to store poisons that eliminates any chance that children or pets can gain access to a poison.*

Evaluation Strategy

In the *evaluation strategy* part of the design plan, designers explain their thoughts behind the evaluation plan; they do not give examples of evaluation tasks.

The evaluation strategy for the poison prevention course is rather simple. It depends on participants working with others in the class while the facilitator moves through the course checking on each participant. The description in the design plan might look like this:

> *This course will use a level 2 peer-to-peer evaluation strategy supported by a facilitator's observations. With an open-enrollment group this large (25 or so), it is unrealistic to expect to implement a more formal evaluation strategy. Given the time limitation (1 hour) and instructional methods, it is necessary to rely on peer interaction to provide the first evaluation and on the facilitator to provide secondary evaluative support. It is anticipated that participants should be able to meet the course objective evaluated with this strategy.*
>
> *The evaluation will take place at the end of the course, when each participant is expected to draw a map of his or her house and identify possible poison danger spots. Working with a peer, each participant will complete his or her map and show it to a partner. Each partner will offer advice and comments for improvement. The facilitator will answer questions as he or she visits each group.*
>
> *Participants will complete a level 1 evaluation to measure their reactions to the course and the training room environment.*

The design need not go further than the foregoing description to ensure that there is a thorough overview of the evaluation process.

Participant Prerequisites

It is an absolute necessity that participants meet any *prerequisites* for a course they are slated to attend. This gatekeeper process describes entry-level competencies that are necessary to prevent population mismatches in courses. The analysis element of the ADDIE model provides this information about what the prerequisites should be.

Designers have to accept the fact that their prerequisites are not always honored. It is not unusual to see an instructor provide training at a lower level to meet the needs of the lowest common denominator in the target population.

Designers can use a tool known as ranging to widen the gate for a course without throwing the prerequisites away. When designers apply ranging, they are setting the highest and lowest points of entry for participation in the course. They would specify these points in their design.

An example will illustrate how ranging works. Consider a designer who is working on a new word-processing program. An organization is standardizing its software and upgrading it at the same time. There are a number of objectives for the 4-hour course, and most require prior knowledge of the software's previous version. The dilemma is that many people in the target population have no experience with the software because they have been using a different program in their department.

The designer realizes that the new software is not that much different from the software other departments have been using. For the training course, the designer decides to remove some of the more advanced features of the software and provide a general overview of the new software. The prerequisite section of the design plan for the course might read thus:

Participants must have at least 6 months' experience with any word-processing software that includes mail-merge and label-making applications. Participants with less experience will be required to complete the Basic Features tutorial for the new software before attending the course.

Ranging lets designers establish reasonable prerequisites for participants and still provide a path for the learners who cannot meet them. This example showed how ranging would accommodate low-prerequisite learners. Ranging also accommodates overqualified learners.

In the software training example, a small group within the target population has learned the new software on its own. This group does not need the training but does need the certificate to qualify for an upgrade. Ranging can accommodate that population by adding the following sentence to the prerequisite description:

Participants with prior experience on the software have the option of completing a short evaluation to receive the course certificate.

Ranging works well in most situations, although it should not be applied in projects that require a very high level of entrance competencies or prior certification. In these cases, the level of skills necessary at entry are fixed by the demands of the course.

The poison prevention class would have a different type of participant prerequisite description than the software class. Because it has open enrollment, the poison prevention course would have very general prerequisites so as to include many different types of people. The course description might read as follows:

Participants should have an interest in poison prevention and a willingness to participate in small group situations. The course will be delivered in English and requires some basic writing skills at the high school level.

Facilitator Prerequisites

Anyone who has ever attended a course that was facilitated by someone who did not have any substantial knowledge of the subject matter knows how important it is to ensure that facilitators meet certain specifications. These prerequisites allow designers to prepare lesson plans and other materials knowing that facilitators meet a necessary skill level. Designers who add this information to their design plan move their work up a notch in terms of design skills. The specification for the software class might state:

The facilitator must have attended an advanced course in the software and received certification as a facilitator.

For the poison prevention course, the prerequisites for facilitators state:

The facilitator must have attended the 4-hour train-the-trainer program sponsored by the course provider. Those unable to attend the train-the-trainer course may qualify as a facilitator by attending and serving as an assistant facilitator for a minimum of four course presentations.

The foregoing example shows that ranging also works for facilitators. By providing an entryway for potential facilitators who did not attend the train-the-trainer program, the designer has provided a second path by which to meet the qualifications.

Deliverables

In the last section of the design plan, designers specify everything that will be delivered as part of the project. Deliverables are usually tangibles like analytical reports, draft materials, courses on software or other technologies, evaluation forms, and even the design plan itself.

The design plan would specify the following deliverables for the poison prevention course, for example:

- ◆ analysis report
- ◆ design plan
- ◆ draft version of the facilitator's guide
- ◆ draft participant handouts and information sheets
- ◆ draft evaluation instruments
- ◆ final camera-ready copies of all draft materials
- ◆ project evaluation.

How It Looks

OK, let's put everything together in a complete design plan for the Poison Prevention in the Home course. This plan also could serve as a template for design projects in any subject area you choose. Although the content will vary, the basics of great design plans never change. Consider how you might use this design plan.

Figure 10.1. Design Plan for Poison Prevention in the Home

Rationale

Accidental poisonings in the home are a horrifying fact of life in too many families. All it takes to set the scene for this tragedy is for someone to have a short lapse of memory during which the person forgets to close a cabinet door or a container of prescription medication. Those openings can be invitations to a curious child. Accidental poisonings can be easily prevented by implementation of some simple steps. The Poison Prevention in the Home course is designed to provide a quick, powerful lesson in poison prevention for any concerned adult.

Sponsored by a national health-care provider, this course offers a unique method of identifying potential poisoning hazards. Participants draw a map of their residence and highlight the areas that represent poisoning hot spots. Participants make a list of poisons in that location and complete a plan of action for dealing with any hazards. Because poisonings do not always occur in conveniently marked locations around the house, the course employs a secondary strategy for identifying hazards not usually associated with a specific room. Participants then list these hazards and develop a strategy to address those poisons.

This course is implemented in less than 90 minutes, with actual course time set at 60 minutes. The additional 30 minutes are for housekeeping items and a question-and-answer session after the formal class. To allow participant interaction, the anticipated class size is 25 or fewer for each offering.

Handouts, a DVD, and computer-based slides will be provided for each facilitator. A train-the-trainer session will be required for each facilitator before he or she will be certified to implement the course. The target population for this course is adults with an interest in preventing poisoning in their homes.

Target Population

This population is largely adults with a high-school education and an interest in preventing accidental poisoning in their homes. This group will be self-motivated to attend based on the marketing strategy employed by the course sponsor.

Course Description

The poison prevention training is structured and lasts 60 minutes. Instructional methodologies employed include lecture, small group activities, and learner presentation and discussions. The room must be compliant with the Americans with Disabilities Act (ADA) and have the capacity to provide computer projection. Recommended class size is 25 or fewer unless an assistant is available.

Objective

Given handouts, a job aid, and class discussion, the Poison Prevention in the Home participant should be able to create a plan to store poisons that eliminates any chance that children or pets can gain access to a poison.

Evaluation Strategy

This course will use a level 2 peer-to-peer evaluation strategy supported by a facilitator's observations. With an open enrollment group this large (25 or so), it is unrealistic to expect to implement a more formal evaluation strategy. Given the time limitation (one hour) and instructional methods, it is necessary to rely on peer interaction to provide the first evaluation and on the facilitator to provide secondary evaluative support. It is anticipated that participants should be able to meet the course objective evaluated with this strategy.

The evaluation will take place at the end of the course when each participant is expected to draw a map of his or her house and identify possible poison danger spots. Working with a peer, each participant will complete his or her map and show it to a partner. Each partner will offer advice and comments for improvement. The facilitator will answer questions as he or she visits each group.

Participants will complete a level 1 evaluation to measure their reactions to the course and the training room environment.

Participant Prerequisites

Participants should have an interest in poison prevention and a willingness to participate in small group situations. The course will be delivered in English and requires some basic writing skills at the high school level.

Facilitator Prerequisites

The facilitator must have attended the four-hour train-the-trainer program sponsored by the course provider. Those unable to attend the train-the-trainer course may qualify as a facilitator by attending and serving as an assistant facilitator for a minimum of four course presentations.

Deliverables

- analysis report
- design plan
- draft facilitator's guide
- draft participant handouts and information sheets
- draft evaluation instruments
- final camera-ready copies of all draft materials
- project evaluation.

In Conclusion

This chapter explains that the design plan is the detailed description of every aspect of a design project. Plans typically include each of the following elements:

- ◆ rationale
- ◆ target population
- ◆ description
- ◆ objectives
- ◆ evaluation strategy
- ◆ participant prerequisites
- ◆ facilitator prerequisites
- ◆ deliverables.

The chapter defines each of the elements and included examples of how a designer might explain each one in a design plan.

Discussion Questions

1. Why do you think that the design plan is considered the ISD deliverable of choice in professional instructional design projects?
2. Are there any additional elements you would add to the design plan discussed in this chapter?

Chapter 11

Lesson Plans

Chapter Objectives

At the conclusion of this chapter, you should be able to

◆ describe the nine events of instruction

◆ provide examples of each of the nine events.

Almost everyone has heard of a lesson plan, instructor's guide, teaching guide, course plan, or one of the other dozens of terms referring to the teaching tool that a facilitator uses to teach a course. Yet most instructional designers have spent very little time thinking about how lesson plans themselves are designed. There is a great deal of theory and design experience just below the surface when lesson plans are developed using the nine events of instruction.

I think most designers would agree that the single most important aspect of any course design is to see that learners meet mastery. It is equally important that learners are able to carry a skill or concept from the classroom or desktop to application in their lives. To optimize the transfer of knowledge, learners must be able to input, apply, and receive feedback on content in a way that provides a cognitive path to storage in long-term memory. Without this transfer to long-term memory, the act of mastery is a short-lived learner experience.

Over the years, numerous designs for lesson plans have evolved. Although some designers claim that certain plans have their roots planted firmly in a theoretical base, most lesson plans not based on the nine events of instruction are the product of honest efforts that fall well short of reaching professional instructional design standards for course delivery.

The Nine Events of Instruction

The work of Gagne, Briggs, and Wager (1988) is the best source for background information on lesson plan design. One significant aspect of learning theory they describe is the formalization of approaches to designing training. The theory supports the notion that learners are more likely to retain the concepts, skills, and procedures taught to them if they are presented in a way that enhances and supports the way the mind works.

Researchers have been studying how the brain works for years and especially how it retains information. For instructional designers the "how" is an important question. The very essence of the designer's role is to make sure that learners leave with demonstrated mastery of objectives. The nine events of instruction join theory and practice in a way that can be used in most design situations.

Gagne, Briggs, and Wager (1988) built the nine events of instruction on the work of other theorists who studied the way humans process information and move it from sensing to processing to storing in short- or long-term memory. The nine steps in this process and each so-called event have an instructional design component that is critical in lesson plan design. The nine events have application in lesson plans in ways beyond that of lecture and other traditional delivery modalities. Every training intervention must be based on the way the learner processes information, or it just will not work. The nine events are universal in their importance to instructional design.

Here are the nine events of instruction in the author's and Gagne's terminology (see also figure 11.1). To make the nine events more descriptive of their intent, the author has given them new, more literal titles. The terms in parentheses are Gagne's original names for each event.

1. Gaining attention
2. Direction (stating objectives)
3. Recall (recall of prerequisite information)
4. Content (presentation of new material)
5. Application feedback—level 1 (guided learning)
6. Application feedback—level 2 (eliciting performance)
7. Application feedback—level 3 (feedback)
8. Evaluation (assessment)
9. Closure (retention and transfer)

Figure 11.1. Nine Events of Instruction

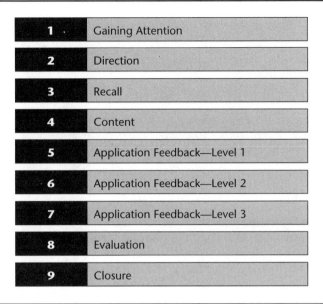

1	Gaining Attention
2	Direction
3	Recall
4	Content
5	Application Feedback—Level 1
6	Application Feedback—Level 2
7	Application Feedback—Level 3
8	Evaluation
9	Closure

Nine Events Repackaged

It is also possible to take a more traditional approach to lesson design and arrange the nine events into three categories, which most people would view as a viable way to assemble a course. In that approach, the categories would follow this format (see also figure 11.2):

A. Preparation for Learning
   1. Gaining attention
   2. Direction
   3. Recall
B. Delivery and Practice of New Material
   4. Content
   5. Application feedback—level 1
   6. Application feedback—level 2
   7. Application feedback—level 3
C. Wrap-Up
   8. Evaluation
   9. Closure (enhancing transfer)

A Close Examination of the Nine Events

Descriptions of the nine events follow. Most of the events include an example that shows how to build a lesson plan using this approach.

Figure 11.2. Nine Events of Instruction Repackaged

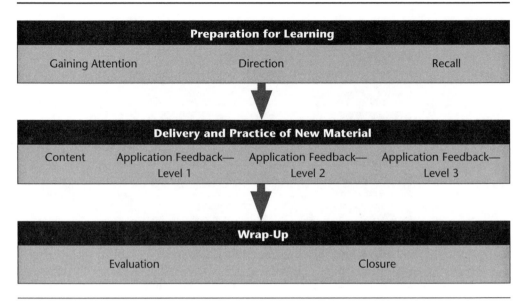

Preparation for Learning

These first three events prepare students to begin the process of learning new content and also provide them with a review of prerequisite information before any new content is delivered. These three steps alone separate the nine events lesson plan approach from other delivery designs.

Gaining Attention

In the beginning of a course, it is necessary to help learners focus on the course. Sometimes gaining attention means setting a tone for the course, whereas other times it means turning off outside interference that is rumbling through a learner's mind. In all cases, the attention-gathering process needs to relate to the topic. A funny story or a joke is not a good attention-getting method as a rule because it can prove distracting, unless a facilitator is certain that it refers to the topic and presents it in a way that is not offensive to the learners. Some methods for gaining attention that have proven effective include the following:

- ◆ playing a video on DVD or audiotapes of 1 minute or less on the topic
- ◆ having a demonstration, such as modeling the task participants will learn in the course
- ◆ role-playing, particularly for addressing affective and interpersonal domain objectives, such as sexual harassment and workplace violence.

Designers should not attempt to start a training program without knowing how the facilitators will gain participants' attention. The designers should let their imaginations go as they search for a way that will start their curricula off with an attention-getting bang.

Consider how a designer might use a video to gain participants' attention during a fictional safety course. (Note that this in no way is meant to be a real course. It is an example for lesson plans.) The course focuses on the increased risks of injury if proper safety procedures are not followed.

1. The designer says, "We are going to open our course with a DVD of a short video highlighting the risks of injury that workers face in certain situations. The workers shown in the video are undoubtedly hard workers like all of us, but safety takes no holidays, and this is a good example of what might happen."

2. Show the DVD—a 1-minute depiction of an accident that injures several workers during routine work.

3. Ask participants what they observed. The designer reiterates the video's point about using proper equipment and procedures.

4. The designer closes by saying, "I think we can all agree that following safety procedures is a necessity for every worker's well-being. None of us wants to be injured or killed on the job."

Direction

The presentation of objectives is a crucial factor in setting the framework for meeting the course objectives. Objectives set the destination so that learners will have a map that shows them where they're going.

Sometimes facilitators or designers say that they want learners to surmise the objectives or that the objectives should be a surprise. Some facilitators or designers ask learners what they would like to learn in a course. If there are any examples of instances in which these methods are successful, they are rare indeed! As chapter 9 described, objectives are the nucleus of all other aspects of instructional design.

Designers should state their objectives in a way that works for their audience. At this stage, they have already completed the audience analysis, which provides the direction for designing the objectives.

For the worker's safety lesson example, the designer needs to set the direction for the participants early in the course, just as any designer would with any project. Stating the objectives in the second event acts as a stabilizing force in the lesson plan. The designer should take the time to think through what it is he or she wants the learners to be able to do and what they should be able to do at the end of that particular session. Following is one approach the designer might take:

1. The designer might say something like the following: "The risks of injury on the job are a matter of life and death. They involve every one of us."
2. "Before you leave, you should be able to identify the potential risks of injury you face on the job."
3. "You should be able to demonstrate how to conduct checks for unsafe conditions."
4. "You should be able to describe how to report unsafe working conditions to a supervisor or union representative."

Recall

To set the context for the objectives, facilitators must prime the learners for the new material by following the three warm-up elements—that is, gaining attention, direction, and recall. It often takes a little bit of information to get learners thinking about the course content and objectives.

In some cases, the recall session may end up being technical to assure the facilitator that participants are ready to move to the new material. Other times, it may be no more than a simple question or discussion that builds the foundation for the information that follows.

One design necessity of this prerequisite element is that it levels the playing field for the facilitator. Depending on content and course design, participants who lack the necessary competencies need assistance. A simple solution that works with some designs is to provide a simple handout or give a brief review. A more thorough review may be necessary if there is a large gap in knowledge or enough of the participants are having problems with the prerequisites.

Designers need to think through this aspect of their design. Effective designs build in options for the facilitators that allow them to add information as necessary once they determine a group's level of competency. For example, they could prepare to give participants handouts with prerequisite content and hold a group discussion that covers the content. The discussion would work well in affective and interpersonal domain objectives.

Facilitators who find that one or more of the participants appear to be struggling with the prerequisite information could distribute a basic handout to provide them with a reference for the rest of the module. Facilitators should be aware that such handouts, although they enlighten some, may bore others who are somewhat familiar with the subject matter and find prerequisite information as stimulating as reading yesterday's paper for the second time.

Facilitators who determine that one or more of the participants are competent enough to assist them with the class should sign them up for that role. They could have those participants circulate through the room, answering questions as necessary.

A pretest for review is a sound design practice. Instructional designers who are unsure of their population's entry competencies should screen potential participants before they attend a course, not after they arrive and expect to participate.

Delivery and Practice of New Material

It is now time to cover the course content and allow students to practice and receive feedback in a safe learning environment. These four elements are the core mechanism for supporting the transfer and storage of the new content into long-term memory.

Content

How content is presented has more impact on learners than any other facet of the design. Implementation is about presenting new material in a way that ensures that learners meet objectives. Designers can be as creative as they wish just as long as they balance this creativity with what their analysis has told them about the learners.

Designers who are presenting highly technical training that resides predominantly in the cognitive domain need to strike a balance between mandated content and its numbing effect on the learners. They must find a way to make everything interesting. Their projects all will be different when it comes to content. They must use their imagination to its full advantage and choose presentation modalities that interest the learner and make the most of the resources available. Following is one example of how to do it, using mining as an example:

1. The instructor may say, "You know your job like the back of your hand, right? So tell me where the danger is in this picture."
2. "All of the pictures you're about to see show areas where there were unsafe working conditions. Some of the problems are more obvious than others are. All of the accidents were preventable. These pictures are also in your handouts."

Application Feedback—Level 1

Instructional designers like to use interactivity when building a course. It is almost as if they have an overwhelming need to allow and encourage participation by learners. The very word "participant" must have evolved from the notion of participation. To be effective, interactivity should not be a question tossed into the room and batted around until something emerges. Designers need to shape and build momentum to keep learners engaged. Application feedback is the point at which designers can give the facilitator and learner an opportunity to begin practicing skills or discussing concepts critical to meeting lesson objectives.

In this first level of application feedback, it is essential that facilitator and learners share equally in the process. One excellent way to do this is to have a large group discussion that involves working though a problem or discussing a concept. It is important that the facilitator involve as many participants as possible in the discussion and draw in those who are holding back. Learners need to have a comfortable environment in which to ask questions. They also need to feel safe enough to experiment and ask a question that, in another environment, they may not ask for fear that it would seem ridiculous.

Application Feedback—Level 2

Individual performance and practice in a safe environment are the main benefits of this event. Learners should now be able to test the waters of the new material. Generally, this portion of the training is built around small-group activities. It is important that learners have an opportunity both to offer and to receive information at this point.

Designers who want interactivity can make it happen during this stage. They should find ways to invite learners into the subject matter and also offer a low-level evaluation of the objective or objectives by both the facilitator and other learners. At this stage of the process, learners are largely on their own and receiving feedback from other learners and the facilitator.

By working in pairs or small groups, learners may ask questions of each other that they might not ask of a facilitator. Designers must provide an easy path from the small group to the facilitator so that learners who are unable to find an acceptable answer among their groups can go to the facilitator for answers and clarification as necessary.

Application Feedback—Level 3

It is really tough for people to make progress if they don't receive any information about how they are doing. This element serves as a learner's friend and partner in training. Avoiding this element produces weak training in both stand-up and technology-driven areas. No substitute exists for midcourse corrections in the learning process. A learner should not be allowed to get to the end of a training event without any information related to meeting the objectives.

First, designers must make sure through the objectives that each learner will get enough feedback about progress to allow correction of any uncertainty or error. A facilitator, another learner, or even a computer could deliver this information. The important thing is that it is delivered.

There are many ways to provide this feedback, and each design's specific objective domains, time limitations, level of difficulty of content, learner variables, and possibly other factors influence each designer's approach. One of the true tests of a good designer is how he or she determines the best feedback scheme for given project.

In the safety example, course participants can review diagrams of their work areas to identify danger spots. A course like this demonstrates how important it is that learners meet objectives. An uncorrected mistake at this point may never get corrected and could eventually have life-threatening repercussions for the learner if an accident occurred.

When thinking about the application feedback elements, it sometimes helps to establish a learner-ownership ratio for the process (figure 11.3). In other words, what percentage of the ownership or responsibility for the learning should a learner have in each of these elements? An ideal ratio in application feedback level 1 is 50 percent instructor and 50 percent learner. This requires the instructor to have the responsibility for the process, but also requires a learner to participate. This often manifests itself in large group discussions or working through exercises as a group with the facilitator in the lead.

Application feedback level 2 is usually 70 percent learner and 30 percent instructor with the learner now taking more responsibility for the learning process. Many times you will see small group discussions, case studies, or role plays in this element since the instructor and learner share the responsibility for the process.

Application feedback level 3 shifts responsibility to the learner and usually sees a facilitator on the sidelines observing and answering questions or correcting errors in content as necessary, but not leading the process. This is where you see presentations by groups or individual learners with a facilitator offering comments or suggestions as feedback. A ratio of 90 percent learner and 10 percent facilitator is ideal.

Figure 11.3. Three Levels of Application Feedback

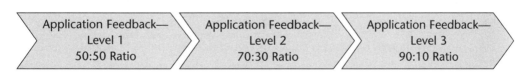

| Application Feedback— Level 1 50:50 Ratio | Application Feedback— Level 2 70:30 Ratio | Application Feedback— Level 3 90:10 Ratio |

Wrap-Up

It is now time to close the learning event by evaluating mastery at a more formal level and bring closure to the experience while also preparing learners for what may follow.

Evaluation

If evaluation is one of the parents of instructional design, then evaluating performance is the first cousin. No learner should leave a training course without passing through an evaluation. This event doesn't always entail a test or other formal evaluation; it is usually just a check-off that ensures that the learner has met the objectives. But every objective has to be evaluated or it isn't worth having as an objective. This is the basis of the performance agreement principle. Objectives have to match evaluation tasks, and it is tough to match these two if one is missing.

Evaluation needs to be a step above simply providing feedback to the learner. It is easy to deliver the evaluation in designs that include a formal evaluation, such as a final test or certification exam. Designers need to find other ways of providing this feedback if they do not plan on offering an exam. For example, for a training program for a sales staff, designers might have a learner simulate closing a sale with a client. They can determine any remaining rough spots and provide the learner with any additional assistance needed to meet the project objectives.

There are several ways that designers could create the final evaluation for the safety class. One way would be for learners to describe to all members of the class the risks in their jobs and present a safety plan to reduce them. This provides one learner with an evaluation and the other learners with ideas that had not been presented before. Most important, the facilitator has the opportunity to comment on the learner's progress and correct any problems that remain.

Closure

During closure, instructional designers need to review the objectives and provide a recap for learners. It is important that learners appreciate the progress they have made and realize that they have met the objectives presented to them at the beginning of the course. The satisfaction of charting progress cannot be overstated. To accomplish these ends, designers have to provide the following during closure:

◆ *Information about any course elements that follow:* Those elements might be the next course in a series or an optional add-on that is being offered. It is vital that the design provide a path to anything that follows. This path is not only for continuity (although it does provide that assistance) but also for prerequisite information so that learners know what to expect next. If learners need to prepare any materials or read anything before attending the next course, they have the necessary information to do that.

◆ *Generalizing information about the knowledge, skills, or abilities provided in the course:* If the content deals with learning to use a 2-quart pot for boiling potatoes, the facilitator might generalize by pointing out that the pot also works for making soup or by explaining two different ways to cook using the same pan. To take another example, in designing a course for attorneys about communication skills for presenting opening arguments, a designer might generalize by showing that attorneys can also use that skill in closing arguments. At a communications level, only the words change, not the process of presenting.

◆ *Synthesizing or finding ways to change the context of the learners' knowledge, skills, and abilities (KSAs):* This skill is to help learners find application of the objectives in a different frame of reference. In the pot example, synthesizing would mean using the pot for catching rainwater. In the attorney communication example, it might mean using that communication skill to argue for a refund at a department store. Synthesizing is important for expanding the dimension of the objectives. Once designers have moved the learner to the target objectives, they can really expand the value of the course.

In the safety example, learners might generalize by encouraging other staff members to look at photographs for dangers in their work areas and at home. The skill has not changed, but it is being generalized to include other areas where workers might confront safety issues. Changing the context of the objectives in this course might mean using a map of the learner's house and expanding it to include other danger zones. This is really using ISD to maximize the impact of the course.

Designing Lesson Plans for Facilitators

Facilitators are the key variable in any instructional design project. A facilitator may also be called a teacher, lecturer, discussion leader, professor, or any of a hundred different titles for the same function, depending on the environment and practice within a learning environment. Facilitation also exists in distance learning and other distributed learning systems. The key factor to remember as an instructional designer when designing lesson plans is that facilitators must be given the right tools to make your design come to life and successfully implement it. The facilitator is as vital to the success of a design project as any other element. The more information designers can provide facilitators, the more likely they are to succeed.

For example, no one likes to get lost while driving. For many people, getting lost evokes feelings of aggravation and stress, and those feelings are only intensified if they are also late. Designers should keep this in mind when they are working on a training project. If they fail to offer facilitators all the information they need to implement the project, they will get lost. The stress associated with facilitating a misdirected training course can have disastrous effects on both the facilitator and the participants.

It is sometimes worse to get skimpy directions than none at all. Right now, a distressed trainer is sitting over coffee somewhere wondering how to deliver an 8-hour course from two pages of an outline. Lesson plans must be complete enough to allow anyone with the necessary subject matter experience to lead the course.

One of the first things designers need to consider as they approach the lesson plan stage of their design work is who their facilitators are. They should consider the following:

- Can the designer identify a range of experience within the pool of potential facilitators?
- Are there any special issues the designer needs to address, such as language or cultural concerns? Will the facilitators require materials in a second language? Does the lesson plan allow facilitators to lead the course in a culturally appropriate way?

The information about the facilitators should appear in the design plan because it aids in the development of the lesson plan.

The Format of the Lesson Plan

Every lesson plan needs to have a format that lends itself to making the implementation of the course as simple as possible. Designers need to use a consistent format if there will be a series of courses. Some stylistic elements that allow for an easy transition from one course to the next include the ideas presented in the following sections.

Each of the nine events is covered in a separate section of the plan, and the title of each usually gets distinctive visual treatment. In the final plan, the name of each event appears in a box along with the suggested time needed for implementing that event. Designers may choose different labels for the sections, but whatever name they use, they should let facilitators know how long each one should take to implement. For example:

> **Gaining Attention—5 minutes**

Notations About Wording

The plan could provide information about what facilitators need to communicate but specify that they should put the information in their own words. The plan might say, for example:

> *In your own words...*
> "In the next hour that we have together, we will learn about working in teams."

The suggested language should be styled so that it is easy for the facilitator to spot it on the page.

Action Items

Action items may be set in boldface type to allow facilitators to see what they are expected to do next, as the following examples show:

Show slide #78.
Start the DVD.

Elimination of Events

Occasionally, designers choose to eliminate events. Sometimes there just isn't enough time for them to go through all of them. Other times nine events may be too complex for a particular project. When designing computer-based training (CBT) or multimedia, it can be difficult to design the necessary feedback and interaction steps. Designers may then decide they can reduce the nine events to seven or fewer events. Usually guided learning, eliciting performance, and feedback suffer the most in this environment.

Designers should be sure at least to consider all nine events when designing a course. Without this kind of guide for designing their lessons, designers are likely to have an outline of the content and an instructional design with no structure, which is the cardinal sin of instructional design.

Technology and the Nine Events

The nine events become even more important if designers are working on a project that is not a traditional facilitator-led course. Designers who use the nine events as the framework for this type of delivery system can be sure they will at least consider the ramifications of all these elements in their design.

It is important to remember that the nine-events approach to lesson plans is not always appropriate. The technology involved may not permit its use. It takes a great deal of work to build lesson plans this way. After designers use this approach for a while, though, they find that the thought process it stimulates becomes instinctive and that it helps them become better designers even if they never again build a lesson plan this way.

How It Looks

Now let's see what a lesson plan looks like in practice. This is a very basic design (figure 11.4) and lesson plans can range in size from what we have here to hundreds of pages in length with visuals and embedded instructional aids.

Figure 11.4. Lesson Plan for Poison Prevention in the Home

Following is a complete lesson plan for the Poison Prevention in the Home course. You may follow this model as you design a lesson plan for your own course.

Implementation time: 1 hour

Materials: Home Poisoning DVD, flipcharts and pens, sign-in sheets, evaluation forms, one set of handouts, one set of poison prevention brochures, blank paper for drawing maps, and name tags. All materials for learners should be in lots of at least 10 percent more than the anticipated attendance.

Equipment: Laptop computer with the presentation software, computer projector and screen, extension cord, and surge protector.

Room arrangement: Classroom style with tables.

24-Hour Checklist

- *Day before:* Confirm room assignment, confirm equipment list, test laptop and software, check computer projector, confirm all materials are ready.
- *One hour before the course starts:* Confirm all room and equipment needs are met, test the equipment, test the computer and software, check the computer projector and connect it to the computer, test the computer-projection link and readiness.
- *Just before the course starts:* Be sure the DVD and DVD player are ready to be played. Make sure you know which chapter on the DVD you want to begin with so you can play it without further preparation. Be sure the computer and computer projector are operating and that the software is operating.
- *Start of the course:* The instructions to the facilitator can take many forms. This lesson plan uses the nine events as a guide. The first event is gaining attention, for which we are going to show a short video. Following is how the lesson plan will look in the facilitator's guide:

Gaining Attention—4 minutes

Show frame #1, welcome to "Poison Prevention in the Home."

Prestart: Call the group together and start the course.
Introduce yourself and formally welcome the learners.

Advance to frame #2, poison threat.

In your own words...

Poisons are a constant threat in all of our homes. We have become so used to having poisons around us that we seldom pay any attention to their presence.

Advance to frame #3, video teaser.

In your own words...

As we watch this short video, see what happens to the Wilson family when they discover too late the dangers associated with poisons in the home.

Put computer projector on standby.

Show video (3 minutes).

In your own words...

As we work together to lessen the potential danger of poisons in your home, use the Wilson family's sad experience to serve as a warning about how quickly poisons can forever change your life.

Direction—3 minutes

Turn computer projector on.

Advance to frame #4, objectives.

In your own words...

We are going to be spending an hour together this evening, and before you leave you should be able to

- Identify different types of poisons in and around your home.
- Make a list of possible poison danger zones in your home.
- Prepare a map of your home highlighting all of the potential danger spots for poisons.
- Describe the first steps to take in the event of a possible poisoning.
- Contact the National Capital Poison Center.

Recall—5 minutes

Advance to frame #5, poison statistics.

In your own words...

Poisons cause thousands of deaths every year in the United States. It is estimated that a vast majority of these deaths could be prevented.

Advance to frame #6, poison definition.

In your own words...

A poison is defined as any substance that can cause negative symptoms. Even a rash is considered to be a negative reaction when determining if something is a poison.

Advance to frame #7, poison labels and icons.

In your own words...

In this country, poisons are required to be labeled to identify them as a dangerous substance. Several icons can designate a poison, and I am sure that you have seen many or all of these either in your home or at work.

Figure 11.4. Lesson Plan for Poison Prevention in the Home (continued)

As you prepare the poison hazard map for you home, you will need to identify which products actually present a potential hazard. You should never rely solely on labels and icons to identify poisons. It is not unusual for chemicals to be stored in unmarked containers after they have been moved from their original packaging. And, of course, the new container is very unlikely to be correctly labeled.

Advance to frame #8, brochure pages.

In your own words...

In your brochure, on pages 3 and 4, you will see drawings of a number of labels and icons used to represent poisons.

Content—15 minutes

Advance to frame #9, killers.

In your own words...

Your home is a deadly place to live. Under your counters and hiding in your closets are killers. Nestled away in your garage are veteran life-threateners. These killers don't care at all about age, gender, or religion. In fact, they don't even care if you are a human or an animal. They are indiscriminate killers with no boundaries and no conscience.

Advance to frame #10, hiding places.

In your own words...

They are hiding in bottles, cans, and boxes. They are of various sizes and colors, and they all look so harmless as they lay in wait for an unsuspecting victim. They seem so innocent until you have fallen into their trap and succumb to their danger.

Let's look at some of these villains and start exposing them to the public.

Advance to frame #11, types of poisons.

In your own words...

There are four general types of poisons that we are going to investigate tonight. They are household products, drugs, plants, and miscellaneous items.

Advance to frame #12, household products.

In your own words...

Household products that are poisonous include insecticides and vermin poisons, anti-freeze, cleaning products, flea killers, and heavy metals like zinc and lead. Pets are especially endangered by fertilizers.

Advance to frame #13, drugs.

In your own words...

Although all drugs should be considered poisonous, we need to remember that even products commonly left out such as vitamins, acetaminophen, ibuprofen, and aspirin are dangerous to children and animals.

Drugs also present the largest risk of pet poisonings with nearly 75 percent of pet poisonings coming from drugs.

Advance to frame #14, plants.

In your own words...

Plants are not usually considered poisoning risks, but they certainly pose lethal problems for animals. Several examples are Japanese yew, philodendrons, and nightshades.

Advance to frame #15, miscellaneous.

In your own words...

Our final category of poisons includes some more common killers of animals that we don't often think about. Chocolate is dangerous for dogs, and food poisoning from garbage is harmful to all animals.

Advance to frame #16, poison locations.

In your own words...

Now that we have identified some of the poisons we need to be concerned about, let's look at the danger points in our homes that are most likely to present poison hazards.

The most common poison locations are the kitchen, bathroom, garage, and everywhere else in your home. No place is totally safe.

Advance to frame #17, kitchens.

In your own words...

The kitchen is a dangerous place. The fact that we eat and cook there seems to lessen our level of awareness to potential poisoning hazards. Look for ammonia, bleach, dish soap, drain cleaners, furniture polish, and cleaning powders.

Advance to frame #18, bathroom.

In your own words...

Bathrooms are second nature to all of us. We seldom, if ever, think about the poisons we keep there. Almost all bathrooms have at least one serious poison hazard.

Look for cleaning agents, cosmetics, deodorants, over-the-counter medications, prescription drugs, and rubbing alcohol.

Advance to frame #19, garage.

In your own words...

Garages seem like the most common place for poisons, and they usually have a number sitting on shelves and on work benches.

Antifreeze, fertilizer, gasoline, lighter fluids, paint, paint remover, paint thinner, pesticides, rat poisons, and weed killers are just part of the list of poisons our garages may contain.

Advance to frame #20, other places.

In your own words...

Although the other areas in our home are somewhat easier to recognize, the rest of the house still offers plenty of opportunities for poisons.

Cigarettes, matches, plants, and paint chips are just some of the poisoning hazards appearing in almost every home.

> **Application feedback—level 1—10 minutes**

Figure 11.4. Lesson Plan for Poison Prevention in the Home (continued)

Advance to frame #21, making a list.

In your own words...

Now that we have identified the types of poisons we might find in our homes and the places that we might find them, let's look room by room through a typical home and see what poisons we can find.

Which room should we start with?

Work through each room in a typical house and list possible poisons in each room. Using a flipchart, begin to make lists for each room. You may want to ask for a volunteer to help write the lists on the flipcharts. Be sure to offer obviously missing examples, but wait as long as possible for a learner to offer them first. Be sure to look also at the garage and yard.

Application feedback—level 2—10 minutes

Advance to frame #22, making a map.

In your own words...

Now we are going to take poison prevention to your home. One of the most effective ways to identify poison trouble spots is by drawing a map of your house and identifying places where you need to be watchful for problems.

On the paper provided, quickly draw a map of your home. If you have more than one floor, pick the floor likely to have the most hazards. You can later finish your map and draw all of your floors.

Now pick a partner next to you and show the person your map. Look at your partner's map and have your partner look at yours. Offer any comments to your partner about his or her map and have your partner comment on yours. Make sure that your partner has identified all the potential trouble spots. When you get home, use your map to check for poisons, and fix any problems you may have.

Circulate around the room and make sure everyone is following instructions. Assist those needing any help.

Application feedback—level 3—5 minutes

In your own words...

If you have finished working with your partner, make any changes necessary to your map. If you have any questions, please let me know so that I can work with you.

Observe the participants and assist where necessary.

Evaluation—10 minutes

Advance to frame #23, volunteer.

In your own words...

I would like to have one of you show the group your map and describe your hazards.

After you have secured a volunteer, assist the volunteer making the presentation. Answer any questions the volunteer or other participants ask.

In your own words...

Make sure your map looks similar to this one and let me know if I can help you in any way. I will stay after the class and assist anyone who needs help. I don't want you to leave without a map that is going to work to prevent a poisoning in your home.

Thanks for volunteering.

Closure—5 minutes

Advance to frame #24, the poison center.

In your own words...

Before we quit, I want to give you some important information in the event you should face a possible poisoning situation.

First, here is the toll-free number for the National Capital Poison Center: It is 1-800-222-1222 and works from anywhere in the United States.

Advance to frame #25, information.

In your own words...

Here is the information you will need when you call:

- age of patient
- condition of patient
- weight
- health history
- exact name of the product
- size of the container
- strength of the product
- when the poisoning occurred
- amount of the exposure
- personal contact information.

I hope you never have to call the Poison Center, but if you do, you will at least have a good idea of the information you will need to give. All this information is in the brochure that you will take home with you.

Advance to frame #26, good-bye.

In your own words...

Thanks for attending tonight, and please take the time to fill out an evaluation sheet. You can just leave it by the door as you leave.

Be sure to use your maps to make your homes safe from possible poisoning hazards. Good-bye!

Close the session and assist any participants with remaining questions. Be sure all participants have taken a brochure with them.

In Conclusion

This chapter completes the exploration of design. It describes the nine events of instruction, which are steps that guide instructors through the design of an effective lesson plan. The chapter also explains instances in which it may be necessary to reorder or eliminate some steps.

Discussion Questions

1. Do you think there are any instructional design scenarios that would allow changing the order of the nine events?
2. Is it possible that a lesson plan can be developed with more or less than nine elements?

◆　Section V

Quality Control

Chapter 12

Quality Rating for Objectives: The QRO

Chapter Objectives

At the conclusion of this chapter, you should be able to

- ◆ describe the quality control process and identify tools for objectives
- ◆ describe the format for the quality rating for objectives
- ◆ complete a QRO for a four-part objective.

Quality Control in ISD

As you advance your skills as an instructional designer, it will be important to establish a system of quality control that allows an unbiased and objective evaluation of ISD projects. The work you review may be your own, something you have been asked to review for someone else, or the work of your department or employees. Regardless of the source of the work, you need a benchmark for each of your design elements that allows you to gauge quality.

The quality rating evaluation instruments presented in this section of the book are examples of how you can accomplish this task. Whether you choose to use these as they are or modify them to fit your work environment and process, it is important that you elevate your professional skill standards as your experience allows. The very fact that you have a quality review process says much about your approach to ISD and your commitment to professional standards.

Quality Rating Matrices

There are three quality rating instruments making their debut in this book. All are intended to make the process of reviewing ISD projects more organized and standardized. The three matrices are quality rating for objectives, quality rating for design plans, and quality rating for lesson plans.

Each of these quality rating tools is based on the standard instructional design formats appearing in this book. As you review the quality rating for objectives, you'll see that it is based on the A-B-C-D format for objectives. The quality rating for design plans is based on the basic design elements most designers use. The quality rating for lesson plans is based on the nine-events format.

You will probably find yourself modifying these quality control tools to fit your needs. These are meant to get you thinking and then moving toward establishing a quality control process for your work.

Quality Rating for Objectives

Writing objectives is both art and science. As such, it retains the best and worst qualities of subjective and objective thinking on the part of instructional designers. To make the process of reviewing the quality of formal ISD objectives more, well, objective, it helps to have a standard tool for evaluating them. The *quality rating for objectives* (QRO) is just such a tool.

The use of the QRO requires a standard from which to benchmark the quality of each individual objective, whether terminal or enabling. The standard described in this chapter has its genesis in the key elements of an objective as presented in this book. It can be modified for individual settings, but it provides a basis for establishing your own standards either for an organization or as a personal standard for quality.

All the elements of an A-B-C-D objective (audience, behavior, condition, degree) are based on standards that conform to sound practice in ISD. Each of these elements is then assigned a numerical value; when summed, the values should total 100 percent for each objective.

Audience

Although the audience statement of an objective is simple in theory, writing a great audience statement is not always easy. The use of the wording "student," "learner," or "participant" is not always the best choice for an objective. Great ISD practice requires that you be much more specific and actually name the course or population as clearly as possible.

For the QRO, consider the three elements of the audience statement:

◆ *Clarity:* Who is the intended audience? (The term *learner* or another generic term is not sufficiently clear.)
◆ *Format:* How well is the audience statement written? Does it make sense?
◆ *Perspective:* Is it written from the perspective of a single learner, rather than from that of a group, a facilitator, an organization, and so forth?

The matrix in table 12.1 can be used to rate the audience element. The maximum score for an audience statement is 20 percent of the 100 percent total for each objective.

Table 12.1. Rating the Audience Statement of an Objective Using QRO

	Maximum Value (%)	Rating (%)
Clarity	10	
Format	5	
Perspective	5	

Behavior

The behavior statement is the most important element in any objective, and that importance is reflected in the QRO. The elements of importance to use in the QRO are:

◆ *Observable:* Is this a behavior that is tangible, or is it ambiguous?
◆ *Measurable:* Is it possible to measure learner mastery?
◆ *Format:* How well is the behavior statement written? Does it make sense?

Table 12.2 is a matrix for rating the behavior element. The total for this element is 40 percent of the quality rating, a very significant part of the total.

Table 12.2. Rating the Behavior Statement of an Objective Using QRO

	Maximum Value (%)	Rating (%)
Observable	15	
Measurable	20	
Format	5	

Condition

When measuring condition elements, it is important to make sure that each objective has a clear foundation of what will be provided within the learner-objective relationship. An objective lacking in conditions is many times unstable instructionally.

The QRO should address three areas of condition statements:

- ◆ *Clarity:* Are all the conditions clearly defined in the objective?
- ◆ *Comprehensiveness:* Are all the conditions mentioned?
- ◆ *Format:* How well is the condition statement written? Does it make sense?

Table 12.3 depicts the QRO matrix for the condition statement. You can have a maximum of 20 percent for the condition element.

Table 12.3. Rating the Condition Statement of an Objective Using QRO

	Maximum Value (%)	Rating (%)
Clarity	10	
Comprehensiveness	5	
Format	5	

Degree

The value of a degree statement in an objective can never be understated; however, it is one of the most neglected elements in most of the objectives written. Consider these three important elements of degree statements in the QRO:

- ◆ *Clarity:* Is there any doubt about what is expected? Does the objective use any ambiguous language including such "-ly" words such as "safely," "carefully," or "honestly"?
- ◆ *Measurable:* Is the degree statement in a format that is measurable?
- ◆ *Format:* How well is the degree statement written? Does it make sense?

Table 12.4. Rating the Degree Statement of an Objective Using QRO

	Maximum Value (%)	Rating (%)
Clarity	10	
Measurable	5	
Format	5	

The QRO for the degree statement will look something like table 12.4. The degree element has a maximum total of 20 percent.

Format for a QRO

Table 12.5 shows how a QRO might appear in practice.

Table 12.5. Example of Quality Rating for Objectives (QRO)

	Maximum Value (%)	Rating (%)
Audience (A) Clarity	10	
Format	5	
Perspective	5	
	Subtotal (20%)	
Behavior (B) Observable	15	
Measurable	20	
Format	5	
	Subtotal (40%)	
Condition (C) Clarity	10	
Comprehensiveness	5	
Format	5	
	Subtotal (20%)	
Degree (D) Clarity	10	
Measurable	5	
Format	5	
	Subtotal (20%)	
Total (A+B+C+D)	**100% Maximum**	

Variations

It is entirely possible that you might decide to add or subtract elements or to change the rating criteria or ratios on your version of the QRO (table 12.6). You should feel empowered to change anything to match your needs. You will probably want to keep as close to a 100-point scale as possible to make your results consistent and to use numerical values that have a common meaning, such as the 100-percent scale used here.

Table 12.6. Blank QRO

	Maximum Value (%)	Rating (%)
Audience (A) Clarity		
Format		
Perspective		
	Subtotal ( )	
Behavior (B) Observable		
Measurable		
Format		
	Subtotal ( )	
Condition (C) Clarity		
Comprehensiveness		
Format		
	Subtotal ( )	
Degree (D) Clarity		
Measurable		
Format		
	Subtotal ( )	
Total (A+B+C+D)	**100% Maximum**	

In Conclusion

The QRO is an advanced instructional design diagnostic and quality control tool for objectives. Designers should modify this tool to conform to their specific format for objectives.

Discussion Questions

1. Do you think that a quality review of objectives is important to an instructional design project?
2. Is it more difficult to review your own work than that of another designer?

Chapter 13

Quality Rating for Design Plans: The QRDP

Chapter Objectives

At the conclusion of this chapter, you should be able to

- ◆ describe the format for the quality rating for design plans
- ◆ complete a QRDP for a design plan.

The design plan in ISD is the standard document of the profession. Whether you use the format used in this book, or some variation, the standard elements of a design plan are the instructional design equivalent of the blueprint in architecture.

The QRDP (quality rating for design plans) provides a common format to review your design plans and make some very objective judgments relating to the quality of each design plan document. As with all quality rating strategies used here, the specifics of your design elements will only vary with the specifics of your approach and will not diminish the usefulness of this instructional design tool.

Recall that a design plan consists of eight elements:

- ◆ rationale
- ◆ target population
- ◆ course description
- ◆ objectives
- ◆ evaluation strategy

- ◆ participant prerequisites
- ◆ facilitator prerequisites
- ◆ deliverables.

Each element is reviewed and assigned a numerical rating; the total for each design plan should be 100 percent.

Rationale

In reviewing a rationale, you want to consider whether it has met the basic requirements of presenting your project in a way that allows the reader, usually a non-designer, to catch the important elements of your plan. Is your rationale truly a short, concise mission statement that delivers the message you want to convey?

The QRDP rates the following elements of a rationale:

- ◆ *Mission:* Is it clear why this course exists?
- ◆ *Detail:* Does the rationale provide the details of the course, including audience and sponsors?
- ◆ *Format:* Is the rationale well written and as brief as possible? Does it make sense?

Table 13.1 is a matrix to help you rate the rationale element. With a total value of 13 percent, the rationale is an important foundation for a design plan and is weighted to reflect that importance.

Table 13.1. Rating the Rationale Element of a Design Plan Using QRDP

	Maximum Value (%)	Rating (%)
Mission	5	
Detail	5	
Format	3	

Target Population

Defining a population within your design plan is a key element when starting your design. Most of your design decisions, including media, methods, and objectives will flow from this element of the design. Several important elements of the target population are reviewed in the QRDP:

◆ *Clarity:* Is it clear whom the population includes?

◆ *Detail:* How much do you actually know about the population? Is this enough?

◆ *Challenges:* Does this element of the design plan identify specifics—both positive and negative—about this population?

Table 13.2 provides a strategy for rating the target population element. The maximum for the population element is 12 percent of the rating.

Table 13.2. Rating the Target Population Element of a Design Plan Using QRDP

	Maximum Value (%)	Rating (%)
Clarity	5	
Detail	5	
Challenges	2	

Course Description

The course description is the logistics and methods element of a design plan. Make sure that all the detail you need for your project is here somewhere. As a minimum have at least these elements in your ratings:

◆ *Course length:* Is it clear how this course is timed (how long, when, and so forth)?

◆ *Instructional method:* How is this course implemented?

◆ *Materials:* What does the facilitator need in terms of handouts, texts, video, audiovisual equipment, and so forth?

The ratings for the description element within the design plan are shown in table 13.3. The course description represents a maximum of 15 percent of the total.

Table 13.3. Rating the Course Description Element of a Design Plan Using QRDP

	Maximum Value (%)	Rating (%)
Course Length	5	
Instructional Methods	5	
Materials	5	

Objectives

Because objectives are the heart of a design plan you want to make sure they are up to your quality standards. At this point in the quality rating process, you can either use the existing QRO matrix or you can just use the QRDP for more operational elements of the objectives in your plan. For this example we are going to use the latter approach.

- ◆ *Number:* Have you included all of the objectives that are needed for this content?
- ◆ *Format:* Are the objectives in the A-B-C-D format?
- ◆ *Detail:* Do you have both terminal and enabling objectives?

Table 13.4 shows quality rating system for objectives. The objectives have a maximum rating of 12 percent of the total.

Table 13.4. Rating the Objectives of a Design Plan Using QRDP

	Maximum Value (%)	Rating (%)
Number	5	
Format	5	
Detail	2	

Evaluation Strategy

This quality rating element actually involves all of the other elements in your design plan because you want to make sure that you have evaluated both the project and process involved in finalizing your design plan. Possible elements for this matrix include:

- ◆ *Detail:* Have you listed and explained your choices for evaluation (type, forms, and so forth)?
- ◆ *Process:* How will you implement the evaluation?
- ◆ *Thoroughness:* Have you been thorough in your evaluation process? Is it real?

The quality rating for evaluation in a design plan is shown in table 13.5. Evaluations are a maximum of 15 percent of the total rating.

Table 13.5. Rating the Evaluation Strategy of a Design Plan Using QRDP

	Maximum Value (%)	Rating (%)
Detail	5	
Process	5	
Thoroughness	5	

Participant Prerequisites

Prerequisites are important to a design plan, so make sure you have covered all the bases with your plan. Evaluate your participant prerequisites according to these criteria:

- ◆ *Clarity:* Is it clear which prerequisites each participant is required to meet?
- ◆ *Ranging:* Have you listed the highest and lowest recommended prerequisites?

Table 13.6 is a matrix you can use to rate your participant prerequisites in the design plan. Eight percent of the total score for the design plan represents the participant prerequisites.

Table 13.6. Rating the Participant Prerequisites of a Design Plan Using QRDP

	Maximum Value (%)	Rating (%)
Clarity	5	
Ranging	3	

Facilitator Prerequisites

Setting the standards for those who facilitate your course is an important aspect of instructional design. At a minimum you should list the qualifications you expect from a facilitator. Be sure not to use vague wording or ambiguous standards. Elements to consider include:

- ◆ *Minimum standards:* Have you listed your expectations?
- ◆ *Clarity:* Are your standards clear and unambiguous?

Table 13.7 shows a method for rating facilitator prerequisites in a design plan. Facilitator prerequisites comprise a maximum of 10 percent of the total.

Table 13.7. Rating the Facilitator Prerequisites of a Design Plan Using QRDP

	Maximum Value (%)	Rating (%)
Minimum Standards	5	
Clarity	5	

Deliverables

Knowing what is required for a project is a great communication tool for designers in working with both a design team and clients. Make sure you have considered the following:

- ◆ *Thoroughness:* Have you included everything?
- ◆ *Clarity:* Is it clear what each deliverable really is?
- ◆ *Responsibility:* Is it clear who is responsible for each deliverable?

Table 13.8 presents a matrix for evaluating the deliverables portion of a design plan. The importance of deliverables is reflected in the maximum of 15 percent of the total rating.

Table 13.8. Rating the Deliverables Element of a Design Plan Using QRDP

	Maximum Value (%)	Rating (%)
Thoroughness	5	
Clarity	5	
Responsibility	5	

The Format for a QRDP

Table 13.9 shows how a QRDP appears in practice.

Table 13.9. Example of Quality Rating for Design Plans (QRDP)

	Maximum Value (%)	Rating (%)
Rationale		
Mission	5	
Detail	5	
Format	3	
	Subtotal (13%)	
Target Population		
Clarity	5	
Detail	5	
Challenges	2	
	Subtotal (12%)	
Course Description		
Course Length	5	
Instructional Methods	5	
Materials	5	
	Subtotal (15%)	
Objectives		
Number	5	
Format	5	
Detail	2	
	Subtotal (12%)	
Evaluation Strategy		
Detail	5	
Process	5	
Thoroughness	5	
	Subtotal (15%)	

(continued on next page)

Table 13.9. Example of Quality Rating for Design Plans (QRDP) (continued)

	Maximum Value (%)	Rating (%)
Participant Prerequisites		
Clarity	5	
Ranging	3	
	Subtotal (8%)	
Facilitator Prerequisites		
Minimum Standards	5	
Clarity	5	
	Subtotal (10%)	
Deliverables		
Thoroughness	5	
Clarity	5	
Responsibility	5	
	Subtotal (15%)	
Total	**100% Maximum**	

In Conclusion

This chapter describes the QRDP and provides instructional designers a format for evaluating a design plan. Designers should feel comfortable modifying this format to fit variations in design plan formats, remembering to change the values to fit a 100-point scale (table 13.10).

Table 13.10. Blank Example of Quality Rating for Design Plans (QRDP)

	Maximum Value (%)	Rating (%)
Rationale Mission		
Detail		
Format		
	Subtotal ( )	
Target Population Clarity		
Detail		
Challenges		
	Subtotal ( )	
Course Description Course Length		
Instructional Methods		
Materials		
	Subtotal ( )	
Objectives Number		
Format		
Detail		
	Subtotal ( )	
Evaluation Strategy Detail		
Process		
Thoroughness		
	Subtotal ( )	

(continued on next page)

Table 13.10. Blank Example of Quality Rating for Design Plans (QRDP) (continued)

	Maximum Value (%)	Rating (%)
Participant Prerequisites		
Clarity		
Ranging		
	Subtotal ( )	
Facilitator Prerequisites		
Minimum Standards		
Clarity		
	Subtotal ( )	
Deliverables		
Thoroughness		
Clarity		
Responsibility		
	Subtotal ( )	
Total	**100% Maximum**	

Discussion Question

1. Why do you think that the QRDP contains so many elements for evaluation of a design plan?

Chapter 14

Quality Rating for Lesson Plans: The QRLP

Chapter Objectives

At the conclusion of this chapter, you should be able to

- ◆ describe the format for the quality rating for lesson plans
- ◆ complete a QRLP for a standard nine-element lesson plan.

The lesson plan in ISD is a standard document of learning professionals spanning the gamut from kindergarten teachers to corporate coaches. Whether you use the exact format used in this book or some variation, the standard nine elements of a lesson plan are included in this quality rating system. Each of the first eight elements also includes a rating for transition. This rating measures how well one element flows into the following element. Stated otherwise, do all the elements fit together to create a comprehensive whole? This is important because a lesson plan should appear seamless to the learner.

Each of the nine elements of a lesson plan are reviewed and assigned a numerical rating; totaling the individual ratings should yield a maximum of 100 percent for each lesson plan.

Gaining Attention

In this first element, make sure you have started the process of focusing a learner on the task at hand. Is it short but powerful, and does it relate to the formal objectives in your design plan? Consider these criteria as you evaluate this element:

- ◆ *Gains attention:* How well does it begin focusing a learner's attention on the content?
- ◆ *Brevity:* Does it last less than 5 minutes?
- ◆ *Relates to content:* Is there a direct correlation?
- ◆ *Transition:* How well does this element flow to the next?

Table 14.1 shows criteria for evaluating the strength of a lesson plan in terms of gaining the attention of participants. Gaining attention accounts for 12 percent of the total in the QRLP.

Table 14.1. Rating the Gaining Attention Element of a Lesson Plan Using QRLP

	Maximum Value (%)	Rating (%)
Gains Attention	5	
Brevity	2	
Relates to Content	3	
Transition	2	

Direction

This section of the lesson plan is where you present your objectives, so you want to be both clear and complete in the way you do this aspect of your lesson plan.

- ◆ *Objectives present:* Are the program objectives clearly identified?
- ◆ *Clarity:* Is it clear what you are asking learners to do?
- ◆ *Transition:* How well does this element flow to the next?

Evaluate the direction element of your lesson plan using the criteria laid out in table 14.2. Direction accounts for 12 percent of the QRLP.

Recall

This key lesson plan element serves as a safety net for learners, so make sure that key prerequisites are reviewed and any deficits in knowledge or performance are addressed before you start with the new content. Ask yourself these questions:

Table 14.2. Rating the Direction Element of a Lesson Plan Using QRLP

	Maximum Value (%)	Rating (%)
Objectives Present	5	
Clarity	5	
Transition	2	

- *Key prerequisite content covered:* Have you covered all of the necessary prerequisites?
- *Strategies for over- and underqualified learners:* Have you allowed for both over- and underqualified learners?
- *Transition:* How well does this element flow to the next?

Recall constitutes 9 percent of the QRLP total. You can use the matrix in table 14.3 for evaluating the recall element.

Table 14.3. Rating the Recall Element of a Lesson Plan Using QRLP

	Maximum Value (%)	Rating (%)
Key Prerequisite Content Covered	5	
Strategies for Over- and Underqualified Learners	2	
Transition	2	

Content

This is the heart of the lesson plan. Be sure to present the content in an ordered and dynamic format; make it real for your learners.

- *Lively:* Is it more than just boring regurgitation of content?
- *Clarity:* Is the content detailed and clear in the way it is presented?
- *Transition:* How well does this element lead to the next?

Content accounts for 11 percent of the QRLP total. Use the scoring system outlined in table 14.4 for evaluating this element.

Table 14.4. Rating the Content Element of a Lesson Plan Usng QRLP

	Maximum Value (%)	Rating (%)
Lively	5	
Clarity	4	
Transition	2	

Application Feedback—Level 1

Now you are ready to reinforce the content, and at this first level you need to have your facilitation at an equal keel with your learners—a joint engagement of content-related interaction with focused and precise feedback. Consider the following:

- *50:50 facilitator-learner ratio:* Is this an even engagement?
- *Application feedback opportunity:* Is there feedback provided?
- *Clarity:* Is the feedback clear from a learner's perspective?
- *Transition:* How well does this element flow to the next?

Table 14.5 presents a method for evaluating application feedback level 1, which accounts for 13 percent of the QRLP total.

Table 14.5. Rating the Application Feedback—Level 1 Element of a Lesson Plan Using QRLP

	Maximum Value (%)	Rating (%)
50:50 Facilitator-Learner Ratio	4	
Application Feedback—Level 1 Opportunity	4	
Clarity	2	
Transition	3	

Application Feedback—Level 2

At this point you want to start handing off the ownership of the content to the learner. Small group work is an example of an implementation modality.

- ◆ *30:70 facilitator-learner ratio:* Are you handing off ownership to the learner at this point in the lesson plan?
- ◆ *Application feedback opportunity:* Is there feedback provided?
- ◆ *Clarity:* Is feedback clear?
- ◆ *Transition:* How well does this element flow to the next?

Application feedback level 2 accounts for 13 percent of the QRLP total. Break down the scoring of this element as shown in table 14.6.

Table 14.6. Rating the Application Feedback—Level 2 Element of a Lesson Plan Using QRLP

	Maximum Value (%)	Rating (%)
30:70 Facilitator-Learner Ratio	4	
Application Feedback— Level 2 Opportunity	4	
Clarity	2	
Transition	3	

Application Feedback—Level 3

Now is the time to provide learners with almost all of the ownership of the content. Think of this as the pre-evaluation phase of your lesson plan.

- ◆ *10:90 facilitator-learner ratio:* Are learners really in control of the content?
- ◆ *Application feedback opportunity:* Is there feedback provided?
- ◆ *Clarity:* Is the feedback clear from the learner's perspective?
- ◆ *Transition:* How well does this element flow to the next?

Application feedback level 3 accounts for 13 percent of the QRLP total, as shown in table 14.7.

Table 14.7. Rating the Application Feedback—Level 3 Element of a Lesson Plan Using QRLP

	Maximum Value (%)	Rating (%)
10:90 Facilitator-Learner Ratio	4	
Application Feedback—Level 3 Opportunity	4	
Clarity	2	
Transition	3	

Evaluation

Now that learners have had three opportunities to practice the objectives, they are ready for the formal evaluation—if it exists. If not, have you designed a process for facilitators to double-check previous informal evaluations from application feedback elements at levels 1, 2, and 3?

- ◆ *Evaluation present:* Does an evaluation actually take place in this element?
- ◆ *Clarity:* Is the evaluation component clear?
- ◆ *Transition:* How well does this element flow to the next?

Evaluation accounts for 9 percent of the QRLP total. See table 14.8 for a systematic way of assessing the evaluation element of your lesson plan.

Table 14.8. Rating the Evaluation Element of a Lesson Plan Using QRLP

	Maximum Value (%)	Rating (%)
Evaluation Present	5	
Clarity	2	
Transition	2	

Closure

Closure—the final element of a lesson plan—is your last chance to perform a quality check. Make sure you also recap the lesson and apply any opportunities to generalize and synthesize the content from the lesson.

- *Recap of content:* Have you reviewed the objectives?
- *Generalization:* Have you generalized the content?
- *Synthesis:* Have you synthesized the content?

Table 14.9 is a systematic means of evaluating your closure element. Closure accounts for 8 percent of the QRLP total.

Table 14.9. Rating the Closure Element of a Lesson Plan Using QRLP

	Maximum Value (%)	Rating (%)
Recap of Content	4	
Generalization	2	
Synthesis	2	

Format for a QRLP

Table 14.10 brings together the whole QRLP instrument; you could use this or a similar model for evaluating your own lesson plans.

Table 14.10. Example of Quality Rating for Lesson Plans (QRLP)

	Maximum Value (%)	Rating (%)
Gaining Attention Gains Attention	5	
Brevity	2	
Relates to Content	3	
Transition	2	
	Subtotal (12%)	
Direction Objectives Present	5	
Clarity	5	
Transition	2	
	Subtotal (12%)	

(continued on next page)

Table 14.10. Example of Quality Rating for Lesson Plans (QRLP) (continued)

	Maximum Value (%)	Rating (%)
Recall		
Key Prerequisite Content Covered	5	
Strategies for Over- and Underqualified Learners	2	
Transition	2	
	Subtotal (9%)	
Content		
Lively	5	
Clarity	4	
Transition	2	
	Subtotal (11%)	
Application Feedback— Level 1		
50:50 Facilitator-Learner Ratio	4	
Application Feedback— Level 2 Opportunity	4	
Clarity	2	
Transition	3	
	Subtotal (13%)	
Application Feedback— Level 2		
30:70 Facilitator-Learner Ratio	4	
Application Feedback— Level 2 Opportunity	4	
Clarity	2	
Transition	3	
	Subtotal (13%)	

	Maximum Value (%)	Rating (%)
Application Feedback—Level 3		
10:90 Facilitator-Learner Ratio	4	
Application Feedback—Level 3 Opportunity	4	
Clarity	2	
Transition	3	
	Subtotal (13%)	
Evaluation		
Evaluation Present	5	
Clarity	2	
Transition	2	
	Subtotal (9%)	
Closure		
Recap of Content	4	
Generalization	2	
Synthesis	2	
	Subtotal (8%)	
Total	**100% Maximum**	

In Conclusion

This chapter describes the QRLP and provides a format for evaluating lesson plans. The method presented here includes the standard nine elements of a lesson plan. For each of the first eight elements, this QRLP also includes a rating for transition that assesses how well one element flows into the next. Designers can modify this format to fit variations in lesson plan formats, but should change the values to fit a 100-point scale (table 14.11).

Table 14.11. Blank Example of Quality Rating for Lesson Plans (QRLP)

	Maximum Value (%)	Rating (%)
Gaining Attention		
Gains Attention		
Brevity		
Relates to Content		
Transition		
Subtotal ( )		
Direction		
Objectives Present		
Clarity		
Transition		
Subtotal ( )		
Recall		
Key Prerequisite Content Covered		
Strategies for Over- and Underqualified Learners		
Transition		
Subtotal ( )		
Content		
Lively		
Clarity		
Transition		
Subtotal ( )		
Application Feedback— Level 1		
50:50 Facilitator-Learner Ratio		

	Maximum Value (%)	Rating (%)
Application Feedback— Level 1 (continued)		
Application Feedback— Level 2 Opportunity		
Clarity		
Transition		
	Subtotal ( )	
Application Feedback— Level 2		
30:70 Facilitator-Learner Ratio		
Application Feedback— Level 2 Opportunity		
Clarity		
Transition		
	Subtotal ( )	
Application Feedback— Level 3		
10:90 Facilitator-Learner Ratio		
Application Feedback— Level 3 Opportunity		
Clarity		
Transition		
	Subtotal ( )	
Evaluation		
Evaluation Present		
Clarity		
Transition		
	Subtotal ( )	

(continued on next page)

Table 14.11. Blank Example of Quality Rating for Lesson Plans (QRLP) (continued)

	Maximum Value (%)	Rating (%)
Closure Recap of Content		
Generalization		
Synthesis		
	Subtotal ( )	
Total	**100% Maximum**	

Discussion Question

1. Lesson plans can be very detailed and the QRLP takes some time to complete. Why do you think it is so important to use the QRLP in your work to evaluate a lesson plan?

◆ Section VI

Advanced ISD Topics

Chapter 15

The Content Mastery Continuum and the Mastery Tipping Point

Chapter Objectives

At the conclusion of this chapter, you should be able to

◆ describe the content mastery continuum (CMC) concept

◆ list at least three ways to use the CMC in instructional design

◆ define the mastery tipping point concept.

The ability of an instructional designer to accurately determine and chart content mastery is critical to a number of important elements of the ISD process. This applies—at a minimum—to both analysis and evaluation in the ADDIE model. It is sometimes extremely difficult to accurately write objectives, sequence content, and determine appropriate evaluation strategies without this data.

There is a design approach available that takes the guesswork out of this process. The content mastery continuum (CMC) provides designers with a number of tools for making these determinations. When used in conjunction with other instructional design elements, a precise map of learner mastery is available to guide critical design decisions.

The principle behind the CMC is that all learner mastery can be charted along a line or continuum that extends from a theoretical entry point of no mastery to an exit point of demonstrated mastery of a content area. This relates to the progressive nature of learning and the fact that mastery of a skill or concept never happens instantly.

Figure 15.1. Content Mastery Continuum

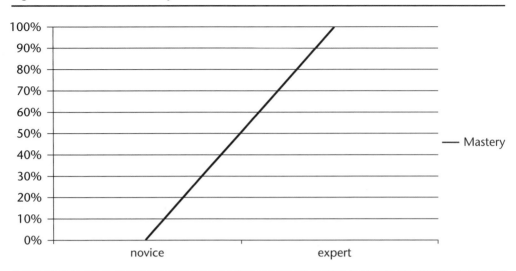

The best way to conceptualize the CMC is to start by reviewing figure 15.1. First look at the point in the lower left-hand corner of the chart labeled *novice*. This point represents a learner or population with no demonstrated mastery of a content area. It starts at the zero percent level of mastery. Now look at the point in the upper right-hand corner of the graph labeled *expert* and corresponding to the 100 percent mastery level. This point represents a learner or population with demonstrated mastery of a content area. In other words, the lower left represents a content novice and the upper right represents a learner with content mastery. The line connecting these two points is the CMC. In all cases, mastery will be somewhere on this continuum from novice to mastery.

Inherent in the design of the CMC is the reality that learners may well have some content knowledge before being involved in a learning activity. The CMC is designed to recognize any relevant content knowledge by allowing a designer to place a learner or a population at fixed points on the continuum based on analysis of the learners. As you will see later in this chapter, this placement provides data for making key decisions concerning prerequisites and content starting points for each specific content area.

The CMC in application is contextual in that it can represent a number of different design scenarios from charting the mastery of a single objective of a single learner to charting an entire population to all objectives within a program.

To chart the CMC for a project, plot specific points of mastery for the learner population at locations along the continuum between novice and mastery. Map the points in sequence from simple to complex since your graph is meant to show clusters of mastery within your population. In practice, the continuum will be divided into as many points as necessary to define your population, with all learners falling somewhere on the continuum for each point of mastery, whether it is defined as an objective or an evaluation task.

The use of the CMC is a process that is usually considered an element in the analysis process and requires some level of data to produce CMC charts. It is possible to use observation and review of readily available evaluation data for this purpose. In some cases it may be necessary to gather data by a more formal analysis process such as pretesting or skills analysis. The strength of the process begins with accurate data; the reliability of the results and value in the design process rests on this foundation.

How the CMC Works

Let's start with a very basic course titled "How to Ride a Bike," which is going to be offered at a local community center. The design team starts by looking at the basic outcomes likely to be associated with this course, namely, the ability to ride a bike without any assistance for a specific period of time, perhaps 10 seconds.

When thinking about terminal objectives for this course, the design team sees three important points of mastery:

1. Skill 1—Mastery of basic safety rules
2. Skill 2—Mastery of preparation and adjustment before riding the bike
3. Skill 3—Mastery of riding for 10 seconds

In the context of the CMC, the team sees three important points of mastery along the continuum from novice to mastery:

1. Safety rules are in the cognitive objective domain and require no prerequisites.
2. Preparation and adjustment are in both the cognitive and psychomotor objective domains and require some prerequisites.
3. Riding is predominately in the psychomotor domain and requires both skills 1 and 2 as prerequisites to attempt mastery of skill 3.

A quick population analysis by the design team shows that the students are not expected to have any significant skills in these three areas, so when they chart the CMC for this course in terms of content mastery, it looks like table 15.1.

As one would suspect, no student has mastery of any of the skills in the course. Students enter as novices, so the design team must plan on covering all of the material in each of the three skill levels.

Table 15.1. CMC in Relation to Content Mastery

Mastery Level	Skill 1	Skill 2	Skill 3
Mastery			
Functional			
Novice	X	X	X

When the team charts the CMC in relation to the objective domains it looks like table 15.2.

Table 15.2. CMC in Relation to Objective Domains

Domain	Skill 1	Skill 2	Skill 3
Cognitive	X	X	
Psychomotor		X	X
Affective			
Interpersonal			

This tells the team that skill 1 can be evaluated with a written or verbal evaluation. Skill 2 must contain both written or verbal as well some observational evaluation, because there are both cognitive and psychomotor objectives. Skill 3 is psychomotor and should be evaluated by an observational approach.

Because this is an elementary course and content area, the results are obvious. But when the CMC is applied over a series of skills in a more complex design environment, the value of the process becomes apparent.

Program-Level CMC

Let's look at an example at the program level in the knowledge content area of physics and the general requirements expected at different levels of education. In this case, we are looking at expected outcomes, so this is considered benchmarking for a general level of academic study. These figures are arbitrary, so don't consider them as anything more than an example.

Figure 15.2 represents a fictional general content mastery chart for the field of physics as an academic discipline in a university. What this shows is that a high

Figure 15.2. Sample Content Mastery Chart for Field of Physics

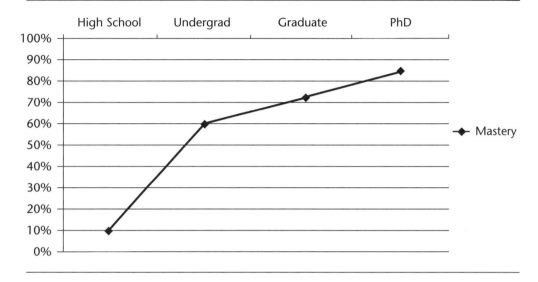

school graduate entering the university has about a 10 percent content mastery of physics. A bachelor's degree in physics offers 60 percent content mastery. A graduate degree offers 72 percent mastery and a PhD indicates an 85 percent or greater mastery of physics. This of course does not relate to any specific subset of content areas, only physics as a general course of study.

Now let's look more closely at this concept at the graduate school program level. We know that the entering graduate students will be entering at approximately 60 percent mastery and that they need to leave the program at a 72 percent mastery in general physics. The graduate program needs to meet that 12 percent expectation in order to meet established standards.

The CMC in Skills Training

Imagine we are designing a course for first responders in a large county fire department. In order to be certified as a first responder, an individual must complete a 40-hour course and then complete two formal evaluations. The first evaluation is a 100-question exam that must be completed with a score of 90 percent or better. In the second evaluation, learners must demonstrate 10 key skills with no errors allowed. Both sections must be completed before a leaner is certified and allowed to assume a first responder role in the fire department.

If we look at this on the individual learner level, we have a CMC chart that looks similar to table 15.3.

Table 15.3. Individual Learner Level CMC—One Learner

Mastery Level	Skill 1	Skill 2	Skill 3	Skill 4	Skill 5
Mastery	X				
Functional		X			
Novice			X	X	X

This CMC chart tells us that this learner has mastery of one skill, functional mastery of one skill, and no mastery of three skills. This tells us that a course in this skill set might easily begin with skill 2 and perhaps skill 1 could be made a prerequisite skill.

Now let's look at table 15.4, a CMC chart for a population of 50 learners in the same content area.

Table 15.4. Population of Learners CMC—50 Learners

Mastery Level	Skill 1	Skill 2	Skill 3	Skill 4	Skill 5
Mastery	36	8	2	1	2
Functional	10	29	15	10	5
Novice	4	13	33	39	43

This population-level CMC chart tells us that our population of 50 learners has 46 learners with at least functional skills in skill 1. This may allow the designer to either make this skill a prerequisite or provide minimal coverage of the skill in a course. Skill 2 has 37 functional or above learners; however, 13 learners have no mastery of this skill. This probably means at least minimal coverage of this skill should be included in a course. Skills 3, 4, and 5 contain enough novices that coverage of these skills is almost mandatory for the course.

The CMC in Analysis

Determining where a population falls for specific points of content mastery can be critical in the analysis process. Once a designer has determined the content required for a course or program, he or she can easily chart the CMC for that population and use that data to make crucial decisions concerning which content to include in the course and which content either can be required as prerequisites or is unnecessary due to mastery already being met by the population.

Table 15.5 is a CMC chart for analysis, which illustrates five specific skills being considered for a particular course. After gathering data, the designer is ready to chart and determine the population's mastery of the five skills. The designer is using the three variable mastery classifications: novice, functional, and mastery. Novice ranking represents a population having little or no mastery of a skill; functional populations are able to reach mastery with assistance; and proficient populations need no assistance to reach mastery. The skills are sequenced from left to right on a continuum from simple to complex within the content area as determined by subject matter experts.

Table 15.5. CMC Chart for Analysis

Mastery Level	Skill 1	Skill 2	Skill 3	Skill 4	Skill 5
Proficient					
Functional	X	X			
Novice			X	X	X

Table 15.5 shows us that the population is functional in skills 1 and 2 and novice in the remaining three skill areas. They are not proficient in any of the skills. This information provides several design options for content inclusion in this course. On one end, skills 1 and 2 could be made prerequisites, and the course could then focus on skills 3, 4, and 5. This would shorten implementation time and perhaps save money. Option two is to simply review skills 1 and 2 and focus most of the course time on the remaining three skills.

To go one step further, the designer for this example has also determined the objective domain for each skill and has charted that data in table 15.6.

Table 15.6. CMC for Objective Domains

Domain	Skill 1	Skill 2	Skill 3	Skill 4	Skill 5
Cognitive	X	X	X		
Psychomotor				X	X
Affective					
Interpersonal					

Table 15.6 tells us that skills 1 through 3 are predominately cognitive and may lend themselves to online learning or a blended course delivery methodology.

Skills 4 and 5 are predominately psychomotor and may require classroom or on-the-job learning implementation.

Each of these examples only shows five skills in the chart, but this process works for five or five hundred or more skills. In fact, the larger the number, the more valuable it becomes since the skills that need designer attention will jump out from the chart.

The CMC in Evaluation

One use for the CMC is to determine the appropriate type of evaluation for a content area within a program or series of courses within a field of study. Imagine a training program in servicing sophisticated medical equipment for hospitals. Participants in the program must complete six courses of 35 hours each to obtain a certificate. Each course requires demonstrated mastery of specific installation and maintenance skills before a learner is allowed to pass to the next course in the series or be granted a certificate after the last course.

Because these courses contain very complex technical knowledge there is no expectation that a learner will be able to demonstrate mastery of a specific skill in the beginning of the course. It is likely that the early course content is predominately cognitive and requires learners to study information and memorize and contextualize theoretical data. This is necessary since learning the theory of how a specific piece of equipment works is required before any training on installation or maintenance is possible.

As the learner moves up the CMC, he or she is building a base for operationalizing of the cognitive theoretical background and learning the more psychomotor aspects of the skill sets such as installation, testing, and maintenance of the equipment. Evaluation necessarily mirrors the CMC because the closer learners get to mastery, the more demonstrated evaluation is required. Simply being able to describe how to service the equipment is of little value unless a learner can demonstrate the required skills. This is the essence of the CMC in evaluation of course and program content. This is where the mastery tipping point comes into play.

We must also recognize that evaluation of content is usually more demanding at the mastery end of the CMC and less demanding at the novice entry point. This relates directly to objective domains and the performance agreement principle.

The Mastery Tipping Point

The mastery tipping point (MTP) is defined as the point on the CMC at which content shifts from one objective domain to another. In our example about servicing medical equipment, the MTP is the point at which the content and evaluation of mastery move from predominately cognitive to predominately psychomotor, and the evaluations move from a learner writing or talking about a process to the learner actually demonstrating skills related to the equipment.

This directly relates to the performance agreement principle in that evaluation must match the intent of the objective in behavior, condition, and degree. If we are evaluating a learner with written or oral tests and the content is specific to a demonstrable skill, we have a serious performance agreement mismatch.

In table 15.7, objectives 1 through 3 for our course are cognitive objectives and objectives 4 and 5 are psychomotor. Our MTP is between objective 3 and objective 4. This tells us that our evaluations must also shift, or we have a performance agreement problem.

Table 15.7. Mastery Tipping Point (MTP) in the Objective Domains

Objective Domain	Objective 1	Objective 2	Objective 3	Objective 4	Objective 5
Cognitive	X	X	X		
Psychomotor				X	X

The evaluations should match the objectives as illustrated in table 15.8.

Table 15.8. Mastery Tipping Point (MTP) and Performance Agreement

Evaluation Domain	Objective 1	Objective 2	Objective 3	Objective 4	Objective 5
Cognitive	X	X	X		
Psychomotor				X	X

If we chart our evaluations and they look like table 15.9, we have a problem that needs to be addressed.

Table 15.9. Mastery Tipping Point (MTP) Indicating a Performance Agreement Problem

Evaluation Domain	Objective 1	Objective 2	Objective 3	Objective 4	Objective 5
Cognitive	X	X		X	
Psychomotor			X		X

In Conclusion

The content mastery continuum (CMC) is a valuable resource for assisting designers in determining the mastery level of either a single learner or an entire population of learners. The CMC represents the entire spectrum of learner mastery on a line or continuum that runs from novice to mastery. By carefully determining learner mastery it is possible to determine prerequisites, evaluation points, and the need to chunk content based on level of achievement.

The mastery tipping point (MTP) is the place within a learning module where evaluation moves from one objective domain to another. This allows designers to determine the precise point in a course where evaluation needs to move to a more rigorous approach to ensure that evaluation is consistent with the intent of the objectives.

Discussion Questions

1. If you are designing a course and the population has significantly different levels of mastery of the intended content, how would you use the CMC to write prerequisites for the course?
2. In a course that contains very technical content, how would you use the mastery tipping point in your course design?

Chapter 16

How to Conduct Focus Groups

Chapter Objectives

At the conclusion of this chapter, you should be able to

◆ define the ways a focus group can support the instructional design process

◆ list the four components of a focus group.

Designing and Conducting a Focus Group

Every instructional designer should be familiar with focus groups and the value they bring to analysis and evaluation. Focus groups range from informal conversations to videotaped productions, and there are almost as many styles as there are designers to facilitate them. The term *focus group* derives from the intent of this analysis tool, which is to focus on a particular topic and capture participants' comments.

Focus groups are used widely for gauging participants' views on such diverse topics as a political issue or a new product that is being brought to market. An instructional designer might be interested in using this tool to determine a population's attitudes about a proposed training strategy or to uncover issues that cause problems in a workgroup.

Regardless of the content or style of a focus group, its single most important component is the facilitator. Each focus group requires a facilitator who remains comfortable if tensions arise (as they surely do) when participants express strong opinions and who is responsible enough to maintain control. It is painful to see an inexperienced facilitator buckle under the pressure of two or more opinionated participants who take over the process.

The model presented here represents the author's experience with these groups in a training setting. Designers will undoubtedly evolve their own strategies and even change them as conditions warrant.

In general, focus groups tend to be useful in data-gathering situations that involve emotions, human interactions, and attitudes. They are also a very powerful problem-solving tool.

Every focus group should have at least four basic components: ground rules, warm-up questions, focus questions, and closers. Following are descriptions of each.

Ground Rules

Ground rules set the code of conduct for the group, in terms of both topic and process. Ground rules should be clearly stated and should appear on an easel sheet or in any other visible place. Common ground rules governing process include time limits on the length of the focus group activity and time limits on individual comments. Topic boundaries include facilitator privilege, such as the authority to moderate as necessary, and confidentiality and non-confidentiality statements.

Time limits are an absolute necessity for most focus groups, although it is sometimes tricky to gauge the time needed to collect data. Time limits assist in focusing participants' thoughts on the topic and help enforce participant and topic boundaries. Typical phrases to use to move the discussion along are "I'm sorry, but we must move on or we will run out of time" or "It sounds like we've hit on a hot topic. We could go on indefinitely, but we have a lot on our plate today; for now we need to move on so that we can meet our session objectives." Individual comments should be limited to 90 seconds or less. Longer comments become speeches, and if one participant is perceived as being in control, others may feel stifled or unimportant. It is sometimes useful to ask participants to think and respond as if they were writing bulleted comments on the topic.

If focus groups are to be a success, it is vitally important to set topic boundaries and enforce them. Facilitators must limit the questions to one or a few topics and let participants know they will be cut off if they wander from them. A focus group concerning workload, for example, can quickly turn into a history of the industrial age. It usually only takes one corrective maneuver to keep that from happening. Facilitator privilege is the right to control the focus group process. The facilitator is the traffic cop of the focus group. There can be no compromise on this component, or the facilitator may quickly lose control of the group.

Confidentiality must also be addressed. The decision to record, transcribe, or otherwise document the group's actions will have an effect on the outcome. Some participants may want comments on record to substantiate a particular view about the topic, whereas others will not feel comfortable saying anything of value if it will be attributed to them. Designers need to discuss these perspectives with a client to eliminate any misunderstanding before the session is held. No matter which choice designers make, they must inform the participants.

Warm-Up Questions

Facilitators usually use warm-up questions to get a group talking and thinking. Some designers call these *framing questions* because they open the gate for participants to enter and frame the rest of the process. Venting is a key element of this early stage of the focus group. Hidden agendas and bottled-up frustrations come to the surface and must be vented or they could damage the focus group. Thirty seconds of griping at this early stage is seldom a problem. Thirty seconds later may negate the entire session.

If a focus group is considering members' attitudes about a new process or procedure, a warm-up question might ask them about their feelings toward change in general. For example, for a focus group about workplace change, the warm-up question might be, "How are things going in the office right now?" or "What is the hot topic of discussion right now?" These warm-up questions start to frame the context of the issue. Immediately the participants know the general direction in which the facilitator is heading. If the participants express tension, anxiety, or anger at this point, the facilitator at least has a barometer of the level of emotion that the topic is generating. Eventually the facilitator will get to the subject, usually with the pressure removed to a degree that allows for an excellent focus group.

Focus Questions

This section is the heart of a focus group. All of the activity before and after supports this group of questions. Designers should first work on these questions as they begin designing their focus groups. Then they can build everything around them. In a group focusing on workplace change, for example, the designer would be interested in the participants' reaction to proposed or suggested changes. The designer might offer a range of options for the groups' reaction, or the designer might build toward one predefined series of changes that an organization might be considering and gauge the participants' reaction. Either way, the focus questions are the most important of all the questions.

If a company is asking about change because it wants to introduce work in teams, for example, the designer might ask, "How do you feel about working in teams?" or "What do you think of the following types of changes?" These questions are different ways of getting to the main point. Facilitators will explore the focus questions in more depth as they begin to gauge the reactions and comments. They sometimes find it useful to narrow the scope of the discussion until they find the level of "no further usefulness."

Closers

A successful close requires a smooth transition. A final question allows participants to bring the topic to closure. Facilitators should ask questions that require some thought and let the participants know that they have been listening to what they say. Here are some examples of closers that include elements of ownership, leadership, and empowerment:

- "If you have the opportunity to say one thing to the boss about this topic, what would it be?"
- "If you were the boss and could do one thing about this situation, what would it be?"
- "You have just been put in charge of fixing this situation, what is your first step?"

Other Focus Group Issues

Some other important issues include attendance by nonparticipants, location, size, and makeup. Many times people are so interested in the process or consider themselves significant enough stakeholders that they demand to be part of the facilitation. This is generally a bad idea, especially if the person sitting in is a stakeholder in the discussion. The presence of a manager or outspoken observer can change the tone of a group. Occasionally, a stakeholder offers input or answers the questions and skews the results of the session entirely.

The location of the focus group process is also important. If a topic is controversial and opinions may be polarized, facilitators should move to a neutral site. The home field advantage is really a disadvantage in some situations. For example, a labor-management topic is best handled on a neutral site to avoid the appearance of managerial influence of the group. Facilitators should not be afraid to move to a new venue if the conditions warrant and the budget allows for it. Even a move across the street to a hotel or restaurant can make the difference between getting what they need or making the problem worse. A move might make participants in a labor-management focus group more willing to say what they are thinking, whereas they might supply stock answers or not participate at all if they are at a stakeholder's environment.

It is important that the focus group resemble the population it is analyzing. Fine-tuning the size and makeup can be a challenge. In some groups this is easy because the focus groups are themselves the entire population. In larger populations, facilitators need to determine which variables are important to the content and assemble their participants in a way that represents those interests. For example, if the population for a focus group on the issue of day care in the workplace is not influenced by age, then age should not be a sampling standard. Gender might very well be a sampling condition. Other qualifiers might be job title, seniority, education, and ethnicity; in fact, anything that might engender a difference of opinion could be a qualifier.

In Conclusion

Focus groups are a key instructional design tool for both analysis and evaluation. The proper format for a focus group will ensure useful results from the process.

Discussion Questions

1. A client is asking that you conduct a focus group with 25 participants. Is this too large a group for an effective focus group?
2. You are conducting a focus group session and it is obvious you have two very different points of view in the group and they are becoming increasingly vocal about their opinions. What should you do?

Chapter 17

The Criticality Approach to Content Selection

Chapter Objectives

At the conclusion of this chapter, you should be able to

- ◆ define the need for a criticality approach to content selection
- ◆ list the four levels of objective criticality
- ◆ list the five criticality rubrics
- ◆ define the key elements of each criticality level
- ◆ provide at least one example for each of the five criticality rubrics.

Making Tough Content Decisions

It is the rare course that has just the right amount of content for time allocated for implementation. It always seems as though you either have too little time or too much content. Although some decisions about what goes and what stays are easily made, most are not. If the process is further complicated by such variables as required content or if you have to navigate a minefield of polarizing opinions held by various decision makers, then you have a recipe for chaos. In such situations, ISD can come to the rescue with a logical way to work through content systematically by providing a way to rate each objective or skill using a system that literally allows content to make the tough decisions for you, based on the relationship of the content to the other design elements.

The logic of this approach lies in the way you rate each skill or objective based on several critical values related to the course—specifically, criticality of the content, frequency of application by a learner, and relationship between criticality and frequency of application.

To apply ISD in this process, you need to turn to a system of matrices that provide conclusive data, which can then be used in a way that works within your design environment. It almost makes decisions for you if you let it, or you can simply take the data and use it within a design group for discussion. There are five matrices that together can provide criticality data:

- ◆ Level 1—Criticality
- ◆ Level 2—Frequency of Application
- ◆ Level 3—Rating Plus Frequency of Application
- ◆ Level 4—Ranking
- ◆ Level 5—Disposition.

Let's look and see how each rubric works alone and in concert with others to form the criticality system.

Level 1—Criticality

Table 17.1 is a level 1 criticality rubric for rating each objective or content element based on its level of criticality within the course in one of the following ranges: critical, essential, prerequisite, and ineffectual.

Although you undoubtedly will evolve your own definition of each of these classifications, it might help to look at the range of each of these classifications.

Table 17.1. Level 1 Criticality Matrix

Rating	Objective 1	Objective 2	Objective 3
Critical Objective			
Essential Objective			
Prerequisite Objective			
Ineffectual Objective			

Critical

Critical objectives are those that cannot under any circumstance be omitted from your course. Among them are

- ◆ *mandated critical:* objectives involving required legal or technical content
- ◆ *performance critical:* objectives that because of the severity of the consequences of omission or poor performance must be included
- ◆ *organizational critical:* required for reasons other than mandate or performance, for example, internal political issues, policy, or practice.

Essential

Essential objectives are those objectives that are not critical but are required for a thorough course in the content area. Examples are

- ◆ *skill steps:* detailed content or procedures on a particular skill or concept
- ◆ *objective domain specific:* objectives that match a required domain requirement, for example, teaching learners specifics of a skill rather than just providing an overview.

Prerequisite

Prerequisite objectives cover content that is sometimes marginal in terms of necessity for implementation but is useful as background information or for ensuring learning conformance with prerequisites. Examples include the following:

- ◆ *relevant policy, practice, or organizational procedures:* setting the background
- ◆ *skills review:* equations, safety rules
- ◆ *adjunct information:* background readings, history, or added detail on a topic.

Ineffectual

Ineffectual objectives are just about every other objective you may have and are not always easy to eliminate. This classification can cause distress in group or team settings where decisions need to be made to shorten a course and issues other than content are involved. For example,

- ◆ *loyalty content:* the video of the organization's president adds nothing to the course
- ◆ *political content:* objectives that are clearly meant to aid organizational presence but offer little or no tangible content.

Level 2—Frequency of Application

In this rubric, shown in table 17.2, you measure the relative value of specific objectives based on the application of the content by a learner. This value is averaged over a population with the acceptance that each individual learner will apply this content in somewhat different ways.

Level 3—Criticality and Frequency of Application

It is now time to combine the criticality and frequency of application data into one rubric (table 17.3), providing you with another dimension for comparison of objectives. It is important to include this additional data rubric because critical objectives that are used most often by learners will trend toward the high range on

Table 17.2. Level 2 Criticality Matrix—Frequency of Application

Application	Objective 1	Objective 2	Objective 3
Daily			
Weekly			
Monthly			
Quarterly			
Yearly			
Never			

Table 17.3. Level 3 Criticality Matrix—Criticality and Frequency of Application

Objective 1	Critical (3)	Essential (2)	Prerequisite (1)	Ineffectual (0)
Daily (5)				
Weekly (4)				
Monthly (3)				
Quarterly (2)				
Yearly (1)				
Never (0)				

this scale. Similarly, less important objectives that are seldom if ever used by learners trend toward the bottom of the scale.

Level 4—Ranking

Now, using a rubric similar to that shown in table 17.4, you need to rank all of your objectives against each other by using the data from the previous rubric (table 17.3). This process provides you with clear and concise placement for each objective and makes the process of choosing objectives much easier.

Level 5—Disposition

Now is the time to make the final decisions about your objectives and to chart those decisions in this rubric. This rubric, based on the format of table 17.5, will probably be the final worksheet you'll need for preparing your design plan.

Table 17.4. Level 4 Criticality Matrix—Ranking

Ranking	8	7	6	5	4	3	2	1	0
Objective 1									
Objective 2									
Objective 3									

Table 17.5. Level 5 Criticality Matrix—Disposition

Disposition	Objective 1	Objective 2	Objective 3
Mandatory			
Recommended			
Optional			
Work/Job Aid			
Prerequisite			
Precourse Reading			
Postcourse Reading			
Unnecessary			

Working Through an Example

Now you'll have the chance to work through the operation of the criticality rubric system using a real-world example. Let's say that you are going to make critical content decisions for a course entitled "Safety in the Workplace" for first-year apprentices in the building trades.

You have the following terminal objectives to make determinations concerning final disposition in a 4-hour course. For this exercise, draft objective wording will be used because you are still in the early stages of the design process and would not yet have formalized the objectives into four parts (A-B-C-D).

- Objective 1: should be able to state OSHA regulation(s) concerning hard hat use.
- Objective 2: should be able to demonstrate recommended hard hat use.
- Objective 3: should be able to list union/company policy on hard hat use.
- Objective 4: should be able to cite possible types of head injury resulting from failure to use a hard hat.
- Objective 5: should be able to list sources for purchasing hard hats.

Now we will work through the level 1 rubric using our five objectives. Table 17.6 represents a possible scenario for these objectives.

Although you might not agree with my rating for each of these objectives, it is clear that there is a pattern of criticality based on these choices. Objective 2 is considered critical, objective 4 is essential, and the remaining objectives (1, 3, and 5) are considered prerequisite. What this tells us as instructional designers is that we have a clear road map to use for gauging inclusion of objectives. If you have time for implementing all five objectives, you are fine. If there's time for implementing

Table 17.6. Level 1 Criticality Matrix (Safety in the Workplace Course)

Rating	Objective 1	Objective 2	Objective 3	Objective 4	Objective 5
Critical		X			
Essential				X	
Prerequisite	X		X		X
Ineffectual					

two objectives, you also have a clear guide to follow—objectives 2 and 4 will be included, and the remaining objectives would be prerequisites or pre- or postcourse reading assignments.

The level 2 rubric allows you to dig deeper into objectives when the issues are not so clear-cut as those in the first example. Assume that there is some disagreement about the outcome of the first rubric and you need to dig deeper to see which objectives should be included. Now, you will include the frequency of application data for review.

Table 17.7 depicts how we might rate these objectives in terms of the frequency of application.

Now you can see a definite pattern starting to appear for our five objectives. The second objective is also something that a learner will probably use every working day on the job. The other four objectives will probably find less frequent use with one actually having only yearly value in terms of learner implementation. Again, you can argue with my rating, but those decisions can be made as a group and ironed out in the course of the conversation. We have now further refined our content criticality to the point where one objective, objective 2, is by far the most important for this course.

Now, let's make your head swim! We are going to further define each of our objectives using the level 3 rubric, which adds each objective's rating (from the level 1 rubric) and application (from the level 2 rubric), arriving at a final, multi-dimensional criticality.

Table 17.7. Level 2 Criticality Matrix—Frequency of Application (Safety in the Workplace Course)

Application	Objective 1	Objective 2	Objective 3	Objective 4	Objective 5
Daily		X			
Weekly					
Monthly	X		X		
Quarterly				X	
Yearly					X
Never					

Table 17.8 shows the rubric completed for objective 1, which we rated as prerequisite (criticality) and monthly (frequency).

As you can see, we added the two values from the first two matrices and came up with a rating of 4 for this objective. Tables 17.9 through 17.12 show the level 3 criticality matrices for the remaining four objectives.

Table 17.8. Level 3 Criticality Matrix—Rating + Frequency of Application (Safety in the Workplace Course, Objective 1)

Objective 1	Critical (3)	Essential (2)	Prerequisite (1)	Ineffectual (0)
Daily (5)				
Weekly (4)				
Monthly (3)			4	
Quarterly (2)				
Yearly (1)				
Never (0)				

Table 17.9. Level 3 Criticality Matrix—Rating + Frequency of Application (Safety in the Workplace Course, Objective 2)

Objective 2	Critical (3)	Essential (2)	Prerequisite (1)	Ineffectual (0)
Daily (5)	8			
Weekly (4)				
Monthly (3)				
Quarterly (2)				
Yearly (1)				
Never (0)				

Table 17.10. Level 3 Criticality Matrix—Rating + Frequency of Application (Safety in the Workplace Course, Objective 3)

Objective 3	Critical (3)	Essential (2)	Prerequisite (1)	Ineffectual (0)
Daily (5)				
Weekly (4)				
Monthly (3)			4	
Quarterly (2)				
Yearly (1)				
Never (0)				

Table 17.11. Level 3 Criticality Matrix—Rating + Frequency of Application (Safety in the Workplace Course, Objective 4)

Objective 4	Critical (3)	Essential (2)	Prerequisite (1)	Ineffectual (0)
Daily (5)				
Weekly (4)				
Monthly (3)				
Quarterly (2)		4		
Yearly (1)				
Never (0)				

Table 17.12. Level 3 Criticality Matrix—Rating + Frequency of Application (Safety in the Workplace Course, Objective 5)

Objective 5	Critical (3)	Essential (2)	Prerequisite (1)	Ineffectual (0)
Daily (5)				
Weekly (4)				
Monthly (3)				
Quarterly (2)				
Yearly (1)			2	
Never (0)				

We now need to rank our five objectives based on the last rubric results (table 17.13). This tells us that objective 2 has the highest ranking (8), with objectives 1, 3, and 4 tied for the next highest ranking (4). Objective 5 is a distant last with a ranking of 2.

Table 17.14 shows an alternative priority-ranking rubric with the objectives appearing in order of decreasing priority.

Our final rubric (table 17.15) provides the final disposition for each objective.

Table 17.13. Level 4 Criticality Matrix—Ranking (Safety in the Workplace Course)

Ranking	8	7	6	5	4	3	2	1	0
Objective 1					X				
Objective 2	X								
Objective 3					X				
Objective 4					X				
Objective 5							X		

Table 17.14. Level 4 Criticality Matrix—Ranking (Safety in the Workplace Course, Alternative Ranking)

Ranking	8	7	6	5	4	3	2	1	0
Objective 2	X								
Objective 1					X				
Objective 3					X				
Objective 4					X				
Objective 5							X		

Table 17.15. Level 5 Criticality Matrix—Disposition (Safety in the Workplace Course)

Disposition	Objective 1	Objective 2	Objective 3	Objective 4	Objective 5
Mandatory		X			
Recommended	X		X	X	
Optional					
Work/Job Aid					X
Prerequisite					
Precourse Reading					
Postcourse Reading					
Unnecessary					

In Conclusion

At this point, you have worked through five levels of criticality and resolved the disposition of each objective in this limited sample from a "Safety in the Workplace" course.

Depending on your situation, it may not be necessary to use each of these steps to make decisions; however, you now have the mechanism available to you to work with other designers, SMEs, and clients on these issues. This process works equally well if you are working solo but need to make critical decisions about objectives.

Discussion Question

1. A client is concerned that a criticality review might suggest that certain key content areas might not be as important as the client believes them to be. What do you say in response?

Chapter 18

Designing for Academic Credit

Chapter Objectives

At the conclusion of this chapter, you should be able to

◆ describe at least two general requirements for credit consideration when designing a course

◆ implement a credit review for a design plan

◆ modify a design plan to improve the likelihood of obtaining credit for a course.

One critical value-added element of instructional design, often treated tangentially outside of academic institutions, is to engage a design philosophy that ensures that each course you design has the potential to provide participants with academic credit. This holds true for almost any course that is designed for college-aged and older populations. This is now common practice in the military, apprenticeship, law enforcement, emergency services, and other occupations and content areas that require certification or licensure. It is also now becoming mandatory in almost any professional training targeted for professional populations within organizations seeking a value-added approach to training and education offerings.

Designing for credit begins with the recognition that most occupational and learning activities that adults engage in are worthy of consideration for college credit.

There are countless examples of where individuals with sufficient life experience demonstrate equal or greater skills in a specific area than a college-educated individual with no life experience in the same content area.

This goes well beyond the concept of providing continuing education units (CEUs), sometimes called professional development units (PDUs), which are often a recognition of attendance, not participation or evaluation. These are usually offered for a fee at a ratio of one CEU for each 10 hours of attendance. CEUs are often used in professional training settings where college credit is not an issue for attendees, but in-service training is often required for licensure, for example, for medical doctors, lawyers, and accountants. Their usefulness for credit seeking learners is often limited at best in most situations, because CEUs are not generally accepted by academic programs as credit toward a degree. As with anything academic, there are exceptions to this general rule, and your situation might be different. Investigate thoroughly, and find out what works best for you in any given circumstance.

The Basics of Designing for Credit

Some general rules apply to courses that are designed to be creditworthy. Although there are many variations on this theme, always keep these issues foremost in your design approach:

- ◆ *College-level content:* Make sure that your content is at least at a postsecondary educational level or that a similar course is offered somewhere in an accredited college or university. The easiest way to do this is to review course descriptions from various colleges or universities in the content area you are covering in your course.
- ◆ *Solid objectives using, at a minimum, the A-B-C-D structure:* Excellent objectives always reflect professional course design standards and are recognized as a sign of sound design practice in an instructional designer.
- ◆ *Tangible evaluation tasks that are implemented at the level of the individual student:* This must be more than just a student listening at a conference. You must have real evaluation that links directly to objectives. This is the performance agreement principle in practice. See chapter 9 for more information concerning performance agreement.
- ◆ *Contact hour ratios of at least 15:1 (hours:credits):* This is the standard in many, but not all, situations relating to student seat-time. Ratios for fieldwork are usually much higher, sometimes 1,500:1 or more. If you are working with modules that are less than 15 hours in length, consider

grouping courses into a program that meets the requirement in terms of minimum contact hours. For example, two 8-hour courses might be bundled as a 16-hour program for one credit.

◆ *Materials and texts that are college level in content:* This is always a bit subjective, but make sure that any materials and texts meet an acceptable level of sophistication relative to the content.

◆ *Instructor prerequisites:* Academic institutions usually require that the instructor of record have a degree at least one level above the level being taught (bachelor's for an associate's and master's for bachelor's, for example). There are numerous variations on this requirement in different situations, but it is worth keeping in mind as you design your course.

◆ *Record keeping:* Records must reflect each individual student's attendance, evaluation, and final disposition within the course. These records usually are shared with the academic institution for eventual placement on a student transcript.

◆ *Student participation and competence:* To receive academic credit, courses must have standards for acceptable student participation. This is sometimes a letter grading system or some variation of the pass/no credit grading option. Make sure the student is informed of the grade received.

The design plan is where most of the information relating to creditworthiness appears. The design plan is a reflection of the system that is developed for a course. The elements in the design plan provide the perfect platform for this information and are already uniquely positioned to accept the additional detail for this process. A well-written design plan is vital to this process. Let's look at each element of the design plan as it relates to the design-for-credit philosophy.

Rationale

Because this is the mission statement for your course, there are several elements of your rationale that will support your credit request.

◆ *Organizational purpose:* It is vital that you provide detailed information concerning the organization sponsoring the course, specifically relating to the mission of the organization that includes providing education and training to adults.

◆ *Organizational endorsement:* It must be clear that the organization is sponsoring this course. Identical courses offered by different sponsors are not always identical in the eyes of an accrediting body.

- *Organizational structure:* It must be clear, at a minimum, that the sponsoring group has the capacity for record keeping and other necessary administrative functions.
- *Education goal:* The course should contain material at a postsecondary level.

Target Population

Defining your population is critical to seeking credit. As you identify the target population, keep in mind the following:

- *Age of the target population:* Generally, participants must be at least 18 years old.
- *Application:* You need to make the case that participants will be able to use the course for professional or academic advancement, usually a degree, certificate, or licensure.

Course Description

The detail contained in the course description provides several key elements of information for the process of seeking credits for the course:

- *Implementation time:* The number of contact hours for a course is critical to determining creditworthiness and value. Remember that a ratio of 15:1 (contact hours to credit) is often used as a guideline.
- *Instructional methods:* Be sure to list the different types of methods you will use in your course, including instructor-led learning, case studies, role plays, online instruction, and so forth.
- *Course administration:* Delineate how the course will be implemented in operational terms, including the record keeping elements of attendance and evaluation.
- *Materials:* List all materials including handouts, texts, and formal evaluation instruments.

Objectives

Objectives are the heart of your design plan. Here are several things to remember:

- *Detail:* Make sure your objectives are written in the most detailed way possible.
- *Format:* Do not stray from the A-B-C-D format, because it is a common method of writing objectives in professional and academic environments.
- *Domain:* Be sure to include the primary and any secondary objective domains.
- *Clarity:* Objectives must by measurable and observable—without exception.

Evaluation Strategy

Credit requires evaluation, and this element of your design plan allows you to showcase your evaluation strategy for a course. Although this is a common element of ISD, here are several things to keep in mind while working on evaluation in your plan:

- ◆ *Technique:* Make it painfully obvious how you are going to evaluate learners—detail, detail, and more detail.
- ◆ *Performance agreement:* Every objective must be evaluated and in the resonant objective domains.
- ◆ *Instruments:* Be specific and provide samples of evaluation instruments such as tests, quizzes, or any other method you may employ.
- ◆ *Grading:* Provide detailed information about the grading system you are going to use. Is it pass/fail, letter grade, or audit?

Participant Prerequisites

This key element of creditworthiness should provide the framework surrounding a participant's involvement in a course, including his or her qualifications to enroll and participate. Detailed standards should exist for participation including technical, professional, and educational thresholds.

Facilitator Prerequisites

Always make sure you have provided detailed specifications for those who will be teaching your course, including:

- ◆ *Qualification:* Are there detailed thresholds for facilitation, including education level, certification, experience, relationship to organization, and content?
- ◆ *Documentation:* For documenting qualifications of facilitators, present a plan that fits into the organizational structure of the sponsoring institution.

Deliverables

There's nothing too complicated here—just be thorough. Provide a list of all the deliverables from the course design process, including the design plan, lesson plan, materials, evaluation instruments, and everything else listed in the design plan as a tangible element of the course.

Credit Recommendation Services

Besides the traditional approach of working in partnerships with a college or university to award credit, it is also possible to seek the services of an organization that reviews courses with the potential to offer credit recommendations. Services like National PONSI (http://www.nationalponsi.org/) or the American Council on Education (http://www.acenet.edu/) are two examples. Several thousand regionally accredited colleges and universities honor these credit recommendations, and it is then at the discretion of the academic institution to accept any or all of the credits toward a certificate or degree.

To be accepted for credit, courses must include more than just a great set of objectives. These courses must meet a system of requirements that involves contact hours, requirements for instructors, evaluation, record keeping, content rigor, and numerous other elements that must be met to ensure creditworthiness for a course or program. This is where an instructional designer can easily take the basic ISD deliverables of a design plan and lesson plan and expand them to create the necessary framework for academic review.

Experiential Credits

Many colleges and universities offer credit for life experience, and these credits are often requested through the development of a portfolio that consists of a series of credit requests based on the life experience of the learner. Each essay must contain a college course equivalent and a detailed explanation of why a certain life experience meets or exceeds the requirements of the course in an academic setting. Experiential credit totals are always capped at a set number by the college or university accepting them. These policies are further defined by academic accrediting bodies and state accrediting organizations.

Although experiential learning credits are an important aspect of earning college credits for millions of adults, there is something more that designers can do to help turn learning by adults into credits recognized by many college and universities. Going the extra step of having a course or series of courses reviewed and awarded credit allows learners the opportunity to bring credit to an academic institution that they are attending or request credit through the life experience process.

Partnerships

Many colleges and universities, especially community colleges, are interested in partnerships with apprenticeship programs, businesses, and other organizations that offer them an opportunity to expand their student base. A key ingredient in these partnerships is the courses offered to students by the nonacademic partner.

An excellent example of this relationship is apprenticeship programs offered by building trades unions that are linked to degree programs at an academic partner. Many apprentices now have the opportunity to turn their training into college credit through credit recommendations and partnership programs. There is no reason that this same process can't work for almost every training course.

Academic and experiential credit opportunities through a partnership offer important options for learners. Although the details of how this works in each college or university are generally similar, it is beyond the scope of this book to detail how the credits are accepted (or not) by individual schools, programs, or content majors. Moreover, the cost for moving these credits to a transcript varies widely from one school to another. What is important is that the design process allows the option for courses to be reviewed for credit if that is something that is important to the population the courses will serve.

A credit-for-courses design philosophy includes a system for making sure that academic course requirements are considered at each step in the design process. In most cases, this is not a difficult task because well-designed courses have many of these elements already; it is often just a matter of packaging the data in such a way that each course has the potential to be reviewed for creditworthiness by a credit-granting college or university.

Working With a College or University on Creditworthy Courses

This process can often be accomplished by working directly with a college or university in a partnership that allows courses to be included as part of a specific program within a school. This is often more easily accomplished with a community college. When working in this scenario, the course or courses will have to comply with the requirements of the school and may have to be reviewed by a faculty committee and approved by one or more levels of academic accrediting requirements at the local, regional, or national level.

Two important elements that most potential accrediting bodies require in a course or program are:

◆ *Stability of implementation and content:* In other words, is the same course that is approved going to be offered each time at every location by each facilitator? A credit course needs to have a minimum number of contact hours, evaluation, and content at each implementation. If you have multiple field locations, all must offer the course exactly as approved.

◆ *Record keeping:* How will attendance, evaluation, and facilitator data be gathered and kept?

This is where ISD and having a professional design and lesson plan offer you incredible support in this endeavor. Because your system contains these elements, it is much easier to design for credit right from the start, and you can offer accrediting organizations very persuasive evidence that you will offer a stable and replicable course or program across a variety of facilitators and sites.

One great advantage of using ISD as your design process is that many of the elements of ISD that you use naturally lend themselves to credit standards. The most obvious element of ISD that works well with this process is the body of objectives. Well-written terminal and enabling objectives will go a long way toward providing a credit foundation, and little consideration will be given for credit to courses that do not have a solid set of objectives.

No matter how you intend to move your courses into a credit environment, designing a course around a credit framework gets you a step closer to having credit awarded for learners that successfully complete a course you design. Even if college credit opportunities are not necessarily the focus of your sponsor or population, the structure of your course will be sound if you are designing with creditworthiness in mind.

In Conclusion

This chapter identifies some of the major design elements to consider if you are interested in pursuing credit options for a course design. It is important to remember that even if a course is designed to be eligible for credit, numerous factors including—but not limited to—specific rules and regulations govern the process, and creditworthiness is not in any way a certainty for any course. Since this chapter presents some general guidelines to consider in the process and does not represent any specific institution or situation, you must always take the time to find out what is required in each individual training and education environment and work from those guidelines as you design.

Discussion Question

1. A client has a number of two-day courses that might be a perfect fit for a credit review. Where do you start?

Chapter 19

Learning Management Systems, Distance Learning, and Design Sense

---

Chapter Objectives

At the conclusion of this chapter, you should be able to

- ◆ identify ways to design within the learning management systems (LMS) environment
- ◆ identify several distance learning components you can integrate into your designs
- ◆ list at least three design issues related to distance learning.

The concept of distance learning has been around for at least 300 years, perhaps longer, depending on how you define the term. From the earliest forms of correspondence learning to the latest online course management tools, distance learning is a valuable asset to an instructional designer. It is important to remember that distance learning, from an instructional design perspective, is just one of many settings for training and education. After all, instructional design, at its core, is a system. Any implementation modality, including distance learning, is just one aspect of a design system.

Arriving at a design decision to use distance learning, classroom learning, or some combination requires a design process that involves assessing the advantages and disadvantages of each option available. It is exactly the same decision-making process as any other design project, and you will make the best decision if you weigh a number of important factors including cost, convenience, and access.

There are as many variations on distance learning as there are instructional designers and learners. Implementation does not have to be all or nothing with distance learning; it can also effectively be adjunct to the core instructional methodology by using message boards, online assignment posting, resources availability, synchronous chat rooms, and hundreds of combinations of these and other methods.

Glamorizing distance learning into something more than it is—an implementation method—increases the likelihood that the technology will be selected solely for the iconic value of the technology itself. Distance learning can be very seductive, and falling blindly for a vendor's promises could leave even an accomplished designer with major, unexpected challenges. Just because a learner has access to the Internet and an organization has a network server and a webpage does not mean that distance learning is the best design choice. The seasoned instructional designer considers all aspects of the population, budget, resources, content, objective domains, and performance agreement when deciding how to implement a learning program.

Distance Learning Design Challenges

Important instructional design decisions for distance learning can usually be reduced to essentially the same questions a designer should ask about any implementation; however, it is necessary to expand the complexity of the discussion with distance learning to the degree that questions need to be answered in several key areas.

In this chapter, *distance learning,* or e-learning, refers to some form of online learning requiring that a learner have both a computer and network access (Internet, intranet, dial-up, and so forth). It is beyond the scope of this discussion to go into the different hardware, software, and other specific details of online learning, although we will discuss learning management systems later in this chapter. The important thing to remember is that these specifics will always be changing and what is hot today will be a dinosaur tomorrow. It is the job of a great instructional designer to keep current with the technology while never losing sight of the ISD process. In the end, instructional design is sufficiently dynamic to allow for implementation of any future technologies; they are just another variable in the design equation.

Population

Any distance learning discussion needs to start with the population it is meant to serve. You must determine if your target population is suited for online learning and has a reasonable chance for success in that environment. All other decisions rest on this decision. Keep these factors in mind when evaluating the target population:

◆ *Access to technology:* The digital divide still exists and remains an issue as each new generation of hardware and software arrives on the scene. Dial-up and the newest advances in fiber-optic broadband access are miles distant in terms of speed, much the same as walking compared to taking a plane to a distant destination. Although you can be creative with how you package online content and supplement with digital media such as DVDs and CDs, there are limits on the end user that you must honor.

◆ *Learning styles:* Are your learners predominantly visual or auditory learners? Or, like most populations, are your learners a combination of several styles? Are they well suited to learning online? Are they comfortable with online requirements such as reading online content and posting comments?

◆ *Learning environment:* There are learners who prefer online to classroom instruction, and others who prefer classroom to online. Although the reasons for these preferences vary among learners, in some cases, a blended approach combining aspects of both can accommodate the needs of all types of learners.

◆ *Timing:* If you are going to require synchronous activities (everyone online at the same time), can your population meet at the assigned times? Ten in the evening in New York City is noon in Seoul, South Korea.

◆ *Technical competence:* Are learners able to use the technology to the degree required for successful participation? Everything from keyboarding skills to working around access issues, such as firewalls and different operating systems, can create frustration and affect completion rates.

Cost

The cost of distance learning in today's design environment can range from negligible to enormous, depending on the requirements of a design. A college or university hosting a learning management system for distance learning can quickly get to six figures just to get up and running. On the other hand, there are low-cost solutions if you want to dig around and find a product that meets your design requirements. There are several things to keep in mind:

◆ *Expectations:* Learners have become just as sophisticated as the technologies now available. If an online learning course is perceived as dated because of its interface or usability, learners may be disappointed or frustrated while they participate. If your choice of products isn't state of the art, expect some participants to be disappointed.

- *Production values:* Developing high-end distance learning generally requires expensive resources because such features as animation, audio, video, and editing may be required. Think of the difference in production quality between the average cable-access television program and a high-definition network-produced show. For a more direct example, compare the average user-developed website with the online products from a major Internet organization. Learners will make the comparisons, and your population profile will tell you whether this is an issue for you to consider.

- *Media:* If you are going to incorporate audio or video components into your distance learning design, you need to be prepared for the costs associated with this design choice. Yes, you can use a $50 webcam and microphone, but would the resultant quality meet your client's or population's expectations for a course? Be realistic about technology costs and what you get for your investment.

Content

Certain content areas drive a decision concerning online learning suitability. Here are a couple of things to consider:

- *Objective domains:* Is your content in a domain that requires hands-on or first-person demonstration, either for presentation or evaluation? If so, can you meet this design need using distance learning? The mastery tipping point concept works well for assessing these situations.

- *Migration of content:* Will you need to transpose content from one format to another, for example, handouts and other materials to online accessibility? Can this transposition be accomplished easily and inexpensively?

Evaluation

This can sometimes be a very complicated area of online learning. Keep these issues in mind:

- *Formal evaluation:* If you are required to have formal evaluations for a course, will you be able to provide an accepted environment for that process? Many for-credit requirements demand that you provide a proctored test environment for online courses. Make sure you know what is required in your content and accreditation environment early in the design process so that you do not encounter any surprises later. Finding proctors for a national program is not a small logistical or budgetary issue.

- *Performance agreement:* Can you evaluate your objectives in the same domain in which they are written? For example, if your objectives are in the psychomotor domain, will you be able to evaluate in that domain?

Implementation

When implementing your lesson plan, view these aspects of the design:

◆ *Facilitator workload:* It generally takes more time to facilitate an online course than a similar classroom-based course. While this can be mitigated by design choices, it is still something to keep in mind.

◆ *Synchronous or asynchronous:* If you are going to incorporate synchronous activities, make sure your technology is learner-friendly. Many chat room environments in course-management software leave much to be desired, and these have a way of diverging into off-topic chats unless they are closely facilitated.

◆ *User satisfaction:* Does the implementation mode match the needs of the learner? Is it the best choice?

Learning Management Systems

With the advent of sophisticated online learning programs, the acronym LMS, or learning management system, has come into popular use. An LMS is the software interface that connects the technology with the student and the facilitator. Behind the curtain of an LMS is sophisticated linkage to the Internet, databases, learning resources, email systems, and embedded support for numerous audio and video components that allow for multi-dimensional course support.

Designers need to spend considerable time reviewing and investigating the numerous aspects of each individual LMS since they often differ from one to another in terms of individual elements and how each works within the software. Added to this potential chaos is the fact that each LMS will undergo versioning changes, so sometimes features present in one version will be dropped or significantly changed in the new version. For example, a legacy LMS may contain a webpage option for students to fill in as a short bio for others to review. This is a great design tool for creating community in an online course. A recent upgrade in a popular LMS eliminated this feature and caused some major redesign in courses relying on this tool. This is a very common occurrence, and good design calls for full review of courses when the LMS is updated to a new version.

The LMS contained in most popular online learning systems contain several basic components:

◆ *Course shells:* These are the discrete home for courses that are usually designated by course name and section numbers.

◆ *Course tools:* Typically these are discussion boards, chat rooms or other synchronous communications within the course population, student and instructor blogs and journals, course materials such as texts, course resources including handouts, and communications access such as email and announcements.

- ◆ *Course support:* This is where you will find wikis, glossaries, access to library resources, and other help functions.
- ◆ *Course grading systems:* This is on the online grade book function usually available to students for instant access to progress reports as well as interim and final grades

Of course, an LMS will contain hundreds of features and each of these will vary by version. Make sure your choice in an LMS meets your needs and provides the necessary structure, tools, and support required for your program.

In Conclusion

Convenience is a common motivation for adults who choose to participate in distance learning. All things being equal, this is a reasonable learner expectation. From the delivery side of the distance learning equation, increasing participation, cost, and access are important considerations. It is up to the designer to see that the experience is of equal or better quality than the same content delivered in any other format. It is the designer's obligation to detail the challenges that each choice offers and weigh the advantages and disadvantages of each. At least everyone will be working with the same data for making decisions.

Discussion Question

1. You have conducted an analysis of a potential population for a new series of courses. Your analysis shows that a majority of your respondents prefer classroom-based courses, yet they also indicate that they will probably choose online courses for the convenience. What does this tell you as a designer?

Chapter 20

ISD and Social Media

Chapter Objectives

At the conclusion of this chapter, you should be able to

- ◆ define social media
- ◆ list several uses for social media in instructional design projects.

With technology changing so rapidly and exciting new ways to communicate appearing almost daily, the urge is to try to take the best of these new innovations and harness them for education and training. Online learning has no real history before the 1980s, and the future is hardly predictable in terms of what will work and what will be popular. The recent past illustrates how the use of computers, laptops, netbooks, and now pad technology has quickly found a home in some instructional design projects.

Web 2.0 is the common denominator for all of this change as the Internet migrates from a view-only environment to an interactive environment where everyone who wants to participate has the opportunity to do so. For instructional designers, this opens up an entire new world of opportunities and challenges.

The world of informal learning is rapidly capturing the imagination of instructional designers as they discover that while the basics of ISD aren't going to change, training and education are certainly maturing with the technology. This offers both promise and pause as designers try to balance excitement with the realities of finding where all of this fits on the design landscape.

The opportunities are limitless if you consider the depth of the emerging social networking offerings. The challenges for designers relate to being able to sift through what is available and then manage the urge to use any of these options without first having a firm design fit between the technology, content, and the population.

Facebook, Twitter, LinkedIn, and MySpace are now part of daily life for folks who have access to the technology and want to use it. There is ample interest in design circles to find a home for social networking in training and education. The question remains, as it does for any tool in our design arsenal, does it fit, and if so where?

Experience tells us that rushing into supporting any type of technology has its risks. The first generation of social networking was email, and courses based on email distribution for content and interaction are difficult to find at this point. Not that email isn't a great way to communicate, but it isn't a great way to teach and learn on the scale that is required for most training and education needs. Its primary strength is on the administrative side of the learning process.

We are now tweeting and texting from our phones to a point that it has saturated our senses and we have to pass laws limiting its use while we drive. Some argue that we need to harness social networking technology for our design needs; others argue that we should remain cautious until we see what is reasonably possible and not rush into another dead-end delivery system.

Of course, both sides are correct. There is truth in both the value and the necessary caution we should practice. As designers, we need to have a process to follow to make sure we are making informed decisions about usage.

University of Maryland Baltimore County (UMBC) faculty member Jeannette Campos teaches a graduate course in social media and learning and offers some important insights into her work on the subject. From her perspective, social media is now so ingrained in the way we work and spend our leisure time that designers would be ill advised to ignore the reality of the impact of this open technology. From a design perspective, however, the challenge is to find ways to integrate the current generation of social media tools into course design since the media itself is implementation focused.

Are we looking at new ways to accomplish the more traditional chat or posting functions in online learning, or is there something more here to catch a designer's interest? Jeannette envisions learning environments that capture the power of these communication tools to ease learners into participating and eliminating any student barriers to expression and thought. In design terms, any interface that allows effective and often instantaneous application and feedback learning moments are worth the design challenge to make this worthwhile.

To take this a step further, imagine a course in art history that includes a set of objectives that requires a student to visit museums or art exhibits and apply previously learned content to new works of art. Armed with an appropriate hand-held smartphone or tablet, the student instantly comments, photographs, and asks questions, all the while tethered to a teacher and other students. The classroom suddenly becomes the world and learning becomes something exciting, but more importantly, instantaneous.

The one issue of concern and one that Jeannette raises is making sure that you have a population that can reasonably be expected to obtain and implement any required social media tools. Like any transitional design tool, computers being the most recent example, it takes time to migrate emerging technologies from the very limited early adapter community to mainstream populations. From a design perspective, does your population analysis support the use of one or more of these tools?

The reality is that most of the tools in social media products essentially mimic what is already available in the present generation of learning management systems, albeit at a different level of sophistication. There is nothing new about posting comments and pictures or chatting online; the real challenge is making all of these elements work flawlessly together in a course to the point where the technology is invisible to the learner.

You must then couple this with the way younger generations of learners, or Net Gens, look at the world. In general they have a different set of expectations (Tapscott, 2009), including:

◆ They want customized options and offerings.
◆ They like to work together but want to be treated as individuals.
◆ In a world of social media, they expect transparency and integrity.
◆ They want life to be fun, both at home and at work.

ASTD commissioned a Web 2.0 study sponsored by Booz Allen Hamilton (2010) and came up with a list of reasons for adopting Web 2.0. They suggest that there are a number of benefits associated with this adoption, including:

- knowledge sharing improves
- learning is fostered
- more informal learning opportunities take place
- communication improves
- resources are more easily located and accessed
- collaboration opportunities increase
- relationships are more easily built.

For an instructional designer, this is a wealth of variables to try and mingle with the expectations of existing older generations or learners who aren't tweeting and posting every several hours. The good news is this is nothing new from a design perspective. New is good when designed with the system.

Designing With Social Media

With all of this opportunity comes the temptation to abandon established design standards, and perhaps even push a systems approach a little to the side. But experience tells us that whatever choices we make in instructional design, the process has proven itself worthy of continued use. Learners must still reach mastery, and there has to be a way to measure that success. The road we travel to get there is but one choice we make as designers.

As always, make sure that your population and approaches are in sync. Pay special attention to the depth of social media penetration within your target population to assure yourself that background and experience will support your choices.

Design with the collaboration button firmly pressed. This aids both job retention in the corporate training world and social networking in all environments. Also be ready to find mechanisms for managing the relentless flow of communications that results from having so many options for exchanging ideas and opinions.

It is a brave new world when designing around the latest leap in technology, especially when each new element of this growth peels back another layer of privacy and, potentially, individualism. Transparency requires a very special design mentality that focuses on the individual as a part of something larger and more impersonal.

Moore's Law in technology tells us that computing power doubles every 18 to 24 months (Moore, 1965). The ISD equivalent is that new technologies to support instructional design increase at the same or greater pace.

As designers we must constantly scan the horizon and harvest those new technologies that promise to deliver transparency to the way learners reach mastery. For in the end, the less students think about the process of learning, the more likely they are to be successful at it.

In Conclusion

Social media is an exciting new tool in the instructional design tool kit. And like any ISD tool, it takes a lot of analysis to determine whether it is useful for any specific design application.

Discussion Questions

1. You are working with a client who insists on using social media for an upcoming project. Your population analysis shows that most of the potential students do not use any type of social media at the present time. What are your options?

2. While designing a course using a popular social networking site, you discover that users' personal information may be compromised under certain conditions. How do you balance your desire to use the most recent technology with concerns about possible confidentiality issues?

3. Everyone is talking about the newest social networking tool and suggesting there is a training use for the product. Where do you start thinking about design applications?

◆ Section VII

Tips for Success

Chapter 21

Working with Subject Matter Experts

Chapter Objectives

At the conclusion of this chapter, you should be able to

- ◆ define the different types of subject matter experts (SMEs)
- ◆ list at least five effective ways to work with SMEs.

Subject matter experts, or SMEs (pronounced smeezs), are often an integral part of a design project. Unless a designer is an expert in a wide range of content areas and never requires outside content expertise, learning to build a productive working relationship with SMEs will always pay dividends.

Subject Matter Experts Come in All Shapes and Sizes

You often hear the term *subject matter expert* when a specific content information need arises, but there are actually a number of different classifications of SMEs, and it is important to recognize the differences. There are SMEs who can assist with the ISD process, such as analysts to gather and make sense of data and attorneys to review contracts and issues including intellectual property rights. Even instructional designers can act as SMEs in the ISD process for other designers.

The most likely scenario for most designers is working with SMEs who are content experts and are brought onboard to supply valuable information concerning a topic. It is their knowledge that brings credibility and validity to the content.

While working with a subject matter expert is no different than working with any other team member, many designers express a lack of confidence in their ability to effectively interact with SMEs. There sometimes develops a level of discomfort that is palatable on both sides of the equation. The reality is that SMEs are often also teachers or trainers and feel an entitlement to an opinion about course design issues. On the other hand, instructional designers feel entitled to the last word on these same course design issues, and thus the conflict.

In order to deflect this potential productivity killer, there are several key attitudinal and organizational points that must be recognized and, if necessary, addressed early in the process. Failing to do so can lead to wasted time and effort later in the process.

Choosing Content Subject Matter Experts

The majority of instructional designers work with SMEs who are project-related content experts. Whether you have any choices about who you work with is as variable as the projects you work on. SMEs for a project are usually either chosen by a client based on political or organizational issues or found by an instructional designer. In either case, it is to the benefit of the designer to see that certain criteria for selection of the SMEs are established. There are a number of important factors to be considered in the selection process.

First, determine if the prospective SMEs have recent experience in the content area. On the surface this may seem a rather odd selection criteria, but too often the selection of SMEs for a project is not based on recent experience in the content. Their assignments are sometimes seen as rewards, and it is not uncommon for selections to be made without any detailed analysis. This may leave a designer with someone who is at least one generation away from current experience. Any SME with more than a year or more between actual time on task and participation as a content expert is likely to be less than reliable.

Second, make sure that any SME has relevant experience in the content. In today's complex world of rapid changes in technology and process, data ages very quickly, and a process or skill that was current a year ago may already be considered legacy knowledge and not relevant to your content. Recent experience does not always mean relevant experience. Five years of recent experience within a field of skills does not mean that someone was working with the specific skills you are looking for in your project. A physician who is a family doctor may have years of general experience, but if your course is directly related to trauma center care of accident victims, you are not going to be well served by this expert. Most choices are not that obvious, but they are all equally important decisions about content subject matter expertise.

Third, try to have a mix of novice, experienced, and expert SMEs if at all possible. This allows you to gather data from the entire range of experience levels. This is often useful because experienced content experts often leave steps out of processes because they perform them almost without thinking about the steps. Experienced SMEs are more likely to be detailed and often have more recent experience. A novice (or potential member of the course's population of learners) will almost always ask excellent questions about a process because they are less likely to have detailed knowledge, but they do know what they don't know, and that is vital for a designer who is collecting data for a course covering the data. If you have to leave any of these groups unrepresented, it is probably best to work with the experienced and expert groups.

Fourth, when working with a national, multi-geographical or multi-organizational group, look for as much variety as possible in SMEs. In many areas, regional variations are critical factors in the success of your work. Sometimes it is the simple variations in jargon and the way different regions refer to tools or processes. At other times it is how people in different areas may or may not do the same things in terms of process. For example, groups on the West coast only perform skills a, b, and c, while groups in Canada have to have experience in cold weather skills d, e, and f. Never take for granted that regional variations are not present or important.

Developing a Working Relationship

The best way to be successful with other non-designer professionals in an instructional design setting is to build a solid working relationship. This is true for everyone who becomes part of your extended design team, but is usually most critical with content SMEs.

There can be a certain tension between SMEs and designers, and this is true almost universally, regardless of the content area or the designer. There are several reasons for this, and all must be considered in the equation for building a working relationship.

Tips for Working Successfully with Subject Matter Experts

First, SMEs must be respected for their knowledge and experience. Like most elements of the design process, working with SMEs requires designers to take a neutral stance on personalities, working styles, and other environmental variables. The goal is to get the best product from the process.

Second, recognize that most SMEs have also taught and that many have actually designed training themselves. It is natural for them to feel that their input on the design process is important based on their experience. Designers may see this as competitive or in some way challenging their subject matter expertise. Don't fall into that trap. Listen and make decisions based on your instincts, but remember that there are occasions where a SME has valuable insights into certain design areas.

Third, initiate and negotiate as necessary the ground rules for the relationship. You will find that 15 minutes spent at the beginning of the relationship will save endless hours and sometimes days of stress and misunderstanding later in the design process. If there are clear lines of authority, it is sometimes best to review them early for clarification and make any modifications that might be necessary. Also make sure that the role of the instructional designer is clear to everyone.

Fourth, make sure that the design process, deliverables, and deadlines are clearly explained and that any points of contention are ironed out early. If there are likely to be negotiations concerning any of these, now is the time to initiate that discussion and resolve the conflict before it develops a life of its own that works against the success of the project.

Fifth, work as an instructional designer—never as a SME—while designing. In the same way that a designer doesn't want to be challenged on his or her design expertise, a designer should never challenge a SME on his or her subject matter expertise. Fair is fair. It is often best to just say early and often that your role is as the designer and any questioning of the content is meant for clarification. If there is a problem with the reliability, value, or usefulness of the information you are receiving from a SME, make this a discussion with the client or sponsor. This is true in both internal and external design relationships.

Sixth, make it easy for a SME to be a subject matter expert. The more a designer can put SMEs in a comfort zone with the process, the more valuable the relationship will become. Always make it easy for them to concentrate on their knowledge and experience and not on the design process. Most SMEs really enjoy the process if their participation is seen as appreciated and noncompetitive.

Seventh, communicate constantly with your SMEs. This includes both the times when you are working in direct contact with them, such as during meetings, and when you are working independently of them on other design issues. No one likes to feel out of the loop, and it is often extremely useful to keep in contact with the SMEs even if there is nothing you actually need from them. A little time spent communicating may ease the way for future requests and consensus.

In Conclusion

Subject matter experts are an integral and important element of many instructional design projects. Finding a way to work most efficiently with SMEs will always pay dividends to an instructional designer.

Discussion Questions

1. A client has asked you to make recommendations for subject matter experts for an upcoming project. What criteria will you use to determine the best fit for your work?
2. You are working on a large project, and you are having difficulty getting the necessary time you need with your subject matter experts. Repeated attempts at working directly with the SMEs to set up a meeting are proving impossible. What should you do next?
3. You are getting frustrated with a specific SME who is trying to tell you how to design a course. Even though the SME is only tasked with assisting with content issues, he is still proving to be a major distraction to the project. How should you approach this problem?

Chapter 22

Developing Personal Portfolios and Presentations

Chapter Objectives

At the conclusion of this chapter, you should be able to

- ◆ list several ways that a personal portfolio aids an instructional designer
- ◆ list several elements of presenting design work to a non-design audience.

One element of being a professional instructional designer that often gets neglected is the art of documenting and showcasing your work. Since many designers may change employers or choose to be a consultant or freelance designer over the course of a career, documenting and showcasing design skills becomes a necessary aspect of professional development. This also has the added benefit of allowing you to revisit designs and products that you may have forgotten about or that can add value to a present or future project.

Saving and Storing Your Work

One of the most important elements of this process is actually having a system for cataloging and storing your work. The easiest way to accomplish project storage is by using either banker's boxes or storage bins purchased at a local discount or office supply store. The obvious addition of data on the outside of the boxes will assist in later retrieval.

Keep a Journal

Keep a work journal that lists each course design and any important details associated with your work. This is really important for work that is considered either classified or proprietary by an employer or client since it at least allows for documenting your work. For each entry, note the title, write a brief content overview, and list design details for future reference.

Showcasing Your Work

To showcase your work, pick one or two projects from each type of work you have designed to add to a portfolio that you actually take with you to prospective clients or employers. Having a nice portfolio case for storing them also adds a touch of class to the process.

If you have digital or online work to showcase, find the best way to display the various components of your project in both static visual elements, such as printouts, as well as a working version of the project you can either project or show on a laptop or monitor.

Presenting Your Work to ISD Professionals

Although you would think that presenting to an audience of ISD practitioners would be a somewhat easier task, the truth is that intimate knowledge of the process will usually result in a very thorough scrutiny of your work. For this reason, it is necessary to make sure that the technical aspects of your work are emphasized. Giving the definition of an objective is probably not a good place to start.

When presenting your work to a team of ISD professionals, you will want to emphasize the data that would normally be contained in a design plan, including your work in

- ◆ population analysis
- ◆ objectives
- ◆ delivery methods
- ◆ evaluation tools and processes
- ◆ deliverables like design and lesson plans
- ◆ student materials including handouts and evaluation instruments
- ◆ working with SMEs and other non-ISD professionals.

Presenting Your Work to Non-ISD Professionals

It is sometimes very challenging to present your work to an audience that is not familiar with ISD since you may have to cover the basics of the process and some common jargon before you can even begin your substantive presentation. There is nothing worse than falling in a jargon-laced conversation with folks who don't speak our language. If you are going to be presenting your work to non-ISD groups emphasize the following:

- ◆ ISD process elements in nontechnical terms
- ◆ finished deliverables such as instructor guides and materials
- ◆ evaluation instruments and reports.

Dr. Greg Williams has written an excellent ASTD *Infoline* on professional portfolios that you should read. It's entitled "Build Your Training Portfolio" (*Infoline* Issue No. 0905, May 2009).

In Conclusion

This chapter outlines several reasons why a personal portfolio of an instructional designer's work is important. It also covers several ways to make presentations to different groups more effectively.

Discussion Question

1. You are working with a group of managers for a client, and they appear to be having difficulty understanding your use of terminology. What do you think is wrong?

Chapter 23

Fine-Tuning Your Skills

Chapter Objectives

At the conclusion of this chapter, you should be able to describe the significance of each of the following instructional designer's tools:

- ◆ mental strategies
- ◆ avoidance of role conflict
- ◆ jargon control
- ◆ designer neutrality
- ◆ knowledge of designer types
- ◆ ability to deal with failure
- ◆ thinking big
- ◆ value neutrality.

Advancing Your Skills

Once instructional designers become comfortable with instructional design as a profession, they often quickly rise within the ranks of an organization based on the variety of adjunct skills they bring to the table, not solely their instructional design skills. These same skills enable some designers to start their own design firms and manage both a design process and a business venture. Others rise through the faculty ranks at academic institutions and often accept positions managing curriculum development and designers.

Designers are systems analysts at heart, and the skills required for this type of professional rigor often spill into related skill sets, including project management and leadership. It is for this reason that instructional designers at any career stage should expand their view over the immediate horizon of instructional design and see what other opportunities present themselves. The list of considerations that follows provides a starting point for this discussion, and as such it would serve every designer to scan the immediate environment for opportunities that lend themselves to designer-based skills and professional practice.

Why Learn These Tools?

Once a designer has learned to create a design plan and lesson plan, he or she knows most of what it takes to prepare and present a really great instructional package. But being a great instructional designer also involves knowing some of the rules of the road about working in the profession. These tools help designers go further in their careers by filling in some of the gaps between preparing and presenting an instructional package and working in the profession.

Mental Strategies

One of the most valuable skills any professional develops is the ability to master the processes necessary to that profession. It is the silent churning of the brain that calls forward every relevant bit of data relating to a situation. Some call it sixth sense, others, second nature. Whatever its name, this background of information professionals have about their specific profession sets them apart from everyone else. It develops from both experience and formal instruction.

Police officers realize that one of the most valuable elements of that profession is the sixth sense they acquire about their surroundings after years of experience. That sense is vitally important and actually saves lives in certain situations.

Professionals in any field approach problems differently than the untrained. This is exactly what happens in every facet of life. The tow truck driver changes your tire in the time it would take you to open the trunk. A heating and air conditioning technician pushes one button and resets the fuse on the nonfunctioning heat pump that has been off for the last three cold nights.

Designers gain experience by working in the field with other professionals, just as professionals do in any other occupation. Some fortunate new designers are lucky enough to have mentors to guide them along. Even those who do not get that guidance can find ample opportunities to keep themselves sharp. The apprenticeship approach for designers usually encompasses watching, working, and waiting. The watching and working aspects are obvious, but the waiting may not be. Unless a designer is fortunate enough to work in an organization that is constantly providing opportunities for learning, designers in training spend most of their time waiting—waiting for something new to do or waiting for a new design challenge besides new employee orientation.

This waiting period proves most frustrating for new designers and may dull the design senses, but this is a prime time for designers to focus on important mental strategies by thinking about them and reviewing them in books and articles. As designers develop a tool kit full of these strategies, they can add to their skills regardless of the opportunities for experiential growth.

An example of a mental strategy is the way a designer determines whether a performance problem has a training solution. Billions of dollars are wasted each year trying to remedy problems that cannot be fixed with training interventions. How often will time-management training be used to solve the problem of poor working conditions or a terrible boss? Don't forget the cardinal rule of analysis from chapter 4: Make sure you have a training issue to solve before you provide a training solution.

Another example is designers' focus on objectives, not just on developing goals. A goal for a training course might be improving productivity. An objective might be that the participant should be able to complete all necessary company paperwork without error. See the difference? Goals point you in the right direction, whereas objectives get you there.

Avoidance of Role Conflict

Instructional designers spend an inordinate amount of time attempting to point out to SMEs how much they can contribute to making a project work. It is sometimes difficult for non-designers to accept that expertise in a content area does not directly correlate with curriculum design expertise.

Some of the hardest work for designers is convincing SMEs that they are better off leaving instructional design to the designers. Some would argue that this do-it-all attitude is more pronounced among SMEs in academics than in other professional fields. It is, nonetheless, a real issue for discussion in any training project.

The realization that they can't do it all requires the same mental process that most people go through when they try to fix a plumbing problem. Plumbers say their best service calls are from clients who have first tried to fix stopped-up sinks themselves. When a do-it-yourself plumber finally makes the call to a professional one, the problem is often worse than it was before the amateurs went to work. The plumbers make twice as much money as they would have had they been called at the first sign of trouble, and the homeowner is happy to pay every penny of it. Similarly, when people with no ISD background try to design training programs, their results are unworkable, and they usually end up calling in the training experts.

It may be necessary for designers to have several run-ins with SMEs or their managers before they earn their respect and acceptance as part of the team. They should never take it personally if people question or challenge the value added by the ISD process. Every designer hears these questions. For each project, designers should develop a list of contributions that they will make. This list will help clarify responsibilities and will minimize the likelihood of misunderstandings later. Eventually the issue of role conflict becomes just one more part of the process and is managed easily.

Jargon Control

Have you ever wondered why professionals feel the need to impress everyone with their ability to use big words and profession-related jargon? There should be a study to document every word, acronym, or unintelligible bit of jargon used with the intent to impress or intimidate. Just think back to the last time you were subjected to jargon, and you can understand how destructive it can be to the communications process unless everyone uses the same language. Can anyone explain why lawyers say "pro bono" instead of "free"?

Jargon, like the nine events of instruction or performance agreement, is an important concept in the instructional design profession. Certain terminology is so common to designers that they are apt to use it without being aware that it is special to the field. It is best not to use these terms with anyone not trained in ISD, including managers, clients, and the audience, at any function where the designer is the guest speaker. In short, designers must be careful to use professional jargon only when necessary and never outside the ISD family.

Designer Neutrality

Designer neutrality relates directly to issues of a political nature within an office. Numerous situations will arise in which someone tries to force a curriculum designer to express an opinion in an area not related to design. These occurrences are most common when the clients are predominately internal. The office wars and personality conflicts that besiege every organization are not fertile grounds for designers. In other words, designers should not get involved in non-design issues outside of their functional workgroup.

Neutrality directly relates to credibility. Designers may never get the respect of their client group if they wander too far away from designing. Designers who express an opinion about anything outside the sphere of the project may suggest to clients that they have a personal agenda.

Subject matter is an especially dangerous area for designers to meddle in. A designer can ruin a focus group or client meeting by expressing an opinion about a topic. Suppose a designer is in the middle of a meeting with an internal client on a proposed hot-topic course. Several times the designer has commented on the subject matter in a way that suggests he or she has an opinion. The designer may later have to defend the design because someone thinks the content slants toward the designer's views. Right or wrong, the designer is now part of the problem, and the designer's solutions may lack credibility no matter how well designed the training is.

Designers who are external to an organization really can get dragged through the mud. People involved in office warfare love to have validation, and someone from the outside agreeing with them is usually all it takes to get something started. Just as with internal client situations, designers should stick to design issues and avoid getting in the middle of office wars.

Types of Designers

Instructional designers can get involved in ISD in a number of different ways. It seems that almost every facet of training can take advantage of the benefits offered by this process. No matter which role a designer is in now, there are probably a large number of people in the same position.

Here are several of the roles that designers might play:

- *Designer and manager:* In this role, a designer also has the responsibility for managing all or a portion of a project or projects.
- *Full-time ISD manager:* An ISD manager does little or no design work and manages one or more projects.
- *Full-time designer:* This person does nothing but instructional design.
- *Designer and facilitator:* This individual both designs the course and is the facilitator.
- *Training staff:* This group of training professionals does everything from design to facilitation.
- *Freelance consultant and designer:* This independent contractor works for a number of different employers.
- *Specialist in one or more ISD elements:* This designer concentrates on one element of the ADDIE model, usually analysis or evaluation.

All of these roles and many more represent the varied situations in which designers might find themselves at any given point in their careers.

There are several reasons it is important to consider the different contexts in which instructional designers may work. First, novice designers should have a good grasp of the different possibilities they may face in the field. Second, there is no one right or wrong way to work as an instructional designer. One way is not more pure than another. Third, instructional designers should consider the best fit for a combination of skills and other factors related to job satisfaction. Some may be happier working alone in a small organization than working in a team in a larger setting.

Designers and Failure

In everyone's work life, there are bad days when he or she makes mistakes. Designers are no different. If someone tried to write down every mistake he or she has made as a designer, it would challenge this book in length. Although it may seem unnecessary to mention this in an otherwise upbeat book, it warrants discussion.

Police cadets are often taught that the most dangerous times for police officers are their first 6 months on the job and the last 6 months before retirement. New officers don't have the experience to always know what to do, and experienced officers have survived a long time and think nothing new can happen to them. Similarly, new designers have a greater probability of making mistakes because they lack experience. When they have been a designer for a while, they tend to become complacent and careless.

Recently an experienced designer was participating in several focus groups with high school students that their teachers attended as observers. This group was a little different from the usual population of adults the designer worked with. Forgetting that teachers like to teach, the designer sat in horror as a teacher got up and taught the students a lesson on the topic during the focus group.

That was a bad day for that veteran designer, but the designer did leave with some important lessons: Make sure you have a plan and that everyone is clear on the process and always follows the plan.

It sounds simple, but focus groups can get out of control, and it takes a good facilitator to make them work the way they should. When those bad days come, it is good to remember that everyone goofs or gets complacent now and then.

Thinking Big

One tool that a designer needs to perfect is the practice of universality. To a designer, that means designing as if his or her curriculum will be implemented in a thousand places at once by a thousand different facilitators. Another aspect of this concept is the notion that the designer will never see, meet, or come in contact with anyone who takes a course he or she has designed. This tool is important even if a designer plans to implement the course with a group of participants with whom he or she is familiar. It enables great designers to look outside their safety zone and review every aspect of a project as if the safety net of familiarity were removed.

This second aspect gets us to a very important issue with designers: separating design work from facilitating. Although some designers do actually play both the designer and facilitator roles, they should design the curriculum as if they will never play both roles.

A friend once commented to me that one of the more serious issues in the training environment was the great teacher complex. This malady usually affects facilitators who think they can just stand in front of a group of learners and impart wisdom by the barrelful. Designers need to be cognizant of the great teacher traits in all of us. This malady will keep designers from preparing the kind of design that any facilitator can use. Instead, they will prepare a design for their own use on the assumption that they can handle any situation that might occur while they are facilitating a course. These designers may not consider a wide array of problems as they prepare their plans, including learners who ask questions far off-topic, whether the lesson will run short or long, and whether there is too much or too little content at an inappropriate level for the population. Their disregard for these fundamental concerns is acceptable if no one else will ever use the designs, but that is not always the case. In fact, many designers never actually facilitate their designs.

An important tool in a designer's repertoire is the ability to wear only one hat at a time: designer or facilitator. Never try to wear both at the same time. Confusion can occur when designers tend to rely on their facilitation skills and subject matter knowledge, as opposed to analysis data, as the following example shows. An instructional designer with a computer science background has the responsibility to design and facilitate a course for a common software package. The analysis shows that the facilitators are from within the organization and are good at using computers, but have no background in computer science. For the course, the basis of the training is the designer's subject matter and facilitation skills. Although the designer includes key concepts in the lesson plan, there is very little detailed information about the workings of the program. The designer would have been able to provide that information in class, but the facilitators cannot fill in the blanks missing in the lesson plan. The course flops because the facilitators cannot provide the missing information, and the designer who has the knowledge is not the facilitator.

Every designer should use personal facilitation skills as one component of good design practice but avoid the trap of leaving out key information or instructions based on one's personal ability to facilitate a particular course. It is a much better practice to put too much detail into a course instead of too little. Facilitators can always select from the information offered.

The Value-Neutral Designer

All of us have opinions. These opinions are based on any number of experiences, cultural and environmental influences, and sometimes even the magazines that greet us in the checkout line at the grocery. It is natural to assume that these biases will travel with us as we conduct ourselves as designers. It is important to always maintain a professional distance from these issues. The only opinions in instructional design should be those related to curriculum development, and the closer a designer can stick to that philosophy the more likely a project will avoid the pitfalls of polarization within a workgroup.

The description of focus groups in chapter 4 mentioned the importance of neutrality while facilitating or designing these types of analysis vehicles. The same must be true of the entire process of designing curricula. If a designer wanders at all from the center of the road, focus might be lost.

The designer's tool of neutrality is not a natural instinct for most of us. Most of us must at times exercise a great deal of conscious effort to keep our personal, non-professional opinions to ourselves. Some designers may rightly argue that opinions are the very energy that drove them to be a designer in the first place. That is a legitimate motivation; however, it is important to remember that non-instructional opinions are usually best left out of the process of instructional design.

Designers work in every conceivable type of environment, from the desert heat of Egypt to the top floor of a multinational corporation. Neutrality relates to process and content and in no way negates loyalty to the organization. A designer should stay out of the opinion business except pertaining to design issues.

The following example will show what happens when neutrality is not maintained during the design process. An organization has requested a course on a controversial subject, perhaps sexual misconduct in the workplace. This topic attracts polarized opinions and has tainted the workplace culture. As the designer visits the cafeteria for refills of hours-old coffee, employees ask about the design department's views of the subject. Should the designer express an opinion, the credibility of the design work would be diminished. The designer's efforts would be negated, no matter what opinion the designer expresses.

In Conclusion

In this chapter the role of an instructional designer is explored in a different context. This chapter highlights the more subtle art of working as a project manager, facilitator, and leader. Even the most seasoned designer can profit from a review of the topics in this chapter.

Discussion Question

1. What are the main non-design issues you face in ISD and how do you handle them?

Chapter 24

Going It Alone
as a Designer

Chapter Objectives

At the conclusion of this chapter, you should be able to

- ◆ identify several roles that the solo designer will have to fill
- ◆ construct at least three strategies to assist you when working as a solo designer.

On Your Own as a Designer

There are as many environments in which instructional designers might find themselves as there are designers. One of the realities of instructional design is that designers often find themselves working as a committee of one in the design process and being a SME, materials development specialist, project manager, and every other role possible in the design process. This is often further complicated by the fact a designer may implement his or her own designs.

Working alone is not necessarily a bad thing; in fact, many designers work in this environment, even in large organizations. They may only work collaboratively at certain critical points as a project matures. My informal research shows that many instructional designers are introverts and, as such, feel as comfortable—or more comfortable—working on their own as they do in a group setting.

Because every design project is, by its nature, meant to be implemented in a population that does not include the designer, receiving feedback and input is critical in this design space. This is more than the expected interaction between client and designer (assuming there is a client) because this is usually not a designer-to-designer relationship. What is needed is a process to assure yourself that your design is both viable and sound as reflected by the review of other designers.

There are several important process issues to consider if you find yourself in this position. Although not all of the strategies discussed in this chapter will apply to your situation, it is important that you consider the usefulness of each of these suggestions.

Separate Roles

Simply stated, when in the design process, think and act as an instructional designer. This may seem painfully obvious in theory, but it is much more difficult to achieve in practice because role conflict can potentially influence your design decisions and your final product. Remember that an instructional designer is the project manager in this process. Discussion and arbitration of differing views and perspectives are a natural part of the design process; if a designer working solo ignores alternative possibilities, or fails to conduct a 360-degree scan of the design environment, the final product may suffer.

At this point, you might be saying to yourself, "But I'm working alone. What does this have to do with my situation?" The answer is everything. Having tunnel vision is an occupational hazard in this environment. Allowing yourself the luxury of segmenting your responsibilities makes you more efficient and productive. Let's look at several important aspects of this challenge and what you can do to make it work for you.

Designer Before Facilitator

The most common example of this role conflict is the very different roles of designer and facilitator. While in the design process, always make decisions based on your role as an instructional designer rather than as the implementer of the final product. This doesn't mean you ignore your experience in the classroom or online; it means you integrate your experience into your design. In other words, consult your teacher-self about issues that relate to that area of your experience.

Experience shows that course designs that reflect choices made predominantly from the perspective of a teacher are generally less detailed, less documented, and less likely to contain alternative strategies for issues that might be encountered in implementation than would choices made from the perspective of a designer. The reasons behind this phenomenon are numerous, but the most obvious is that seasoned facilitators can manage most challenges during implementation. Brevity of design reflects internal confidence that might not be justified. This perspective is especially damaging for designers who will not be implementing a course they design.

Leave the Nest for Review and Evaluation

One of the most challenging aspects of working alone is catching less-than-obvious errors and refining the tough elements of your designs. We have all had the experience of having a simple spelling or grammatical error grow wings and take on a life of its own. Working briefly with another solo designer as you write objectives and lesson plans can help you catch errors and identify gaps in these critical elements of your design.

Ideas to Consider

Here are several ways to mitigate the solo designer syndrome:

- Find at least one trading partner who will review your work in exchange for the same from you. Make sure this is an instructional designer at your level of experience or higher, or you may become frustrated with the process. If you can build a group of designers that meets regularly to talk about projects, this is also very useful. ASTD meetings are a perfect place to find other designers interested in the same support.
- Create templates for key design elements so that the process takes a back seat to the product and you can spend your valuable creativity on your design.
- Where practical, let every element of your design sit for at least a day. Problems and solutions almost jump off the screen toward you after a short mental break.
- Don't reach beyond your limitations. Ask for help. Don't be afraid to send an email or call a trusted designer and ask for an opinion.
- Don't spend your time on tasks that can be more efficiently performed by someone else. If something is truly more work than it is worth, find a way to outsource it and build it into the bid next time you have a similar situation. Don't pretend you can do it all.
- Read your copy backward from the end to the beginning. You will be surprised how many errors you can detect this way.
- Always take advantage of the technology and utilize the spelling and grammar checking options in your word-processing software. This seems so obvious, but it is often ignored in the fog of a deadline.
- Back up your work. Because you probably don't have a network and systemwide backup capacity, make sure you have a routine for saving your files either in a fireproof safe or off site in a bank's safety deposit box. Unfortunately, you will probably ignore this advice until you learn the hard way how important this is.

The Rule of a Thousand

You will find it exponentially useful to think of your design projects as having a life that is beyond your control. For this purpose, the rule of a thousand makes this point exceptionally well. Try thinking about your role as the designer in this context: Imagine that every course you design will be implemented in 1,000 places at once, by 1,000 facilitators, in front of 1,000 populations you will never meet. As frightening as this may seem, it can help focus your work as a designer.

The rule of a thousand also helps to clear away role conflict issues associated with a designer designing as a facilitator. This is not to say that your skills in facilitation are wasted or of no consequence; in fact, quite the opposite is true. You must isolate your design and facilitation skills while incorporating your specific experience in implementation in your design process. Nevertheless, as you design, keep in mind that you won't be able to rely on your own abilities as a facilitator to rush in to save a course or make changes on the fly to correct problems.

In Conclusion

This chapter outlines strategies to consider when working as a solo designer. Many designers struggle with the decision to work within an organizational structure or branch out on their own. With these several tips and ideas to consider, any designer can make the leap to working solo.

Discussion Question

1. What is your biggest challenge as an instructional design working alone, and how do you handle it?

Chapter 25

Giving Back:
The Zen of Pro Bono

Chapter Objectives

At the conclusion of this chapter, you should be able to

◆ list several advantages of providing instructional designer work
pro bono.

Pro bono, or work done for the public good at no compensation, is a philosophy and practice that is common in many professional fields. Probably the most visible examples are law and medicine. But the practice of "giving back" is also alive and well in the instructional design community as well. However, it never garners the same level of visibility that other acts of community support seem to muster.

Instructional designers are constantly assisting community groups, schools, and organizations that support children and the disadvantaged with no thought to compensation. It is this spirit of community that guides many designers to bring design skills to the groups that generally need it the most and can afford it the least.

Assisting with a scouting training project or designing a course for senior citizens on how to use cell phones are just two examples of pro bono design projects. There are countless other needs that go unaddressed because most organizations don't realize that such assistance is available. This is where pro bono work as a designer really pays dividends all the way around. You get experience and visibility, and a worthwhile organization moves its interest forward thanks to your efforts.

Offering your services is as simple as taking a good scan of your environment and asking if you can be of assistance. Most organizations have no idea ISD exists or what it can do for them. Many times a simple explanation of the process and examples of what you have done in the past will do the trick. Other times it might take an example of what might be accomplished for a group to appreciate the value of your service.

What seems like a very minor project to you often seems like rocket science to the uninitiated in the ISD process. A simple plan for training might take you an hour and might be priceless to them. Never underestimate the value of a little professional experience lent to a worthy cause. It is comparable to someone having little knowledge of how an automobile works sitting with their disabled car on the side of the road until a good Samaritan comes along and performs a bit of magic in the engine and it starts right up.

Be sure to journal all of your efforts, and don't be afraid to showcase your pro bono work as part of your professional portfolio. Many times the content and type of work you do in this environment is different from your normal work, and to a potential client or employer, this shows both diversity and depth.

In Conclusion

In this chapter, the rewards of giving back to the community are discussed. Many designers find that the time invested in work for clients that would otherwise not have access to this type of professional assistance provides benefits for everyone involved.

Discussion Questions

1. What are the advantages and disadvantages of taking on a client and working pro bono on a project for them?
2. Would you place any limits on a project if you were doing it pro bono?

Wrapping It Up

Practicing as an instructional designer can reveal a dizzying variety of challenges in a constantly changing training and education environment. It sometimes seems as though the practice of ISD changes on a daily basis. Sometimes the focus is on distance learning, sometimes on performance improvement, and at other times the focus is on nothing at all and leaves designers wondering what the next wave of ISD issues will involve.

The truth of ISD and the practice of instructional design is that the basics will always remain the same within the profession. Distance learning and performance improvement are simply new wrinkles in a system that at its heart is based on the simple concept of the ADDIE model and the importance of using a systems approach when working as an instructional designer. The answers in instructional design are as varied as the questions, and anyone who thinks ISD is about predetermined answers or outcomes simply misses the point. ISD is about process, and the product that follows is the result of that effort.

As such, there isn't a single element of instructional design that is too difficult to learn or use. As with any other professional pursuit, mastering a basic set of skills and learning the tricks of the trade bring it all together. The process of designing training may appear easy and uncomplicated to people outside the process. After all, well-designed training does appear seamless and almost effortless to the observer as it is being implemented. That is one of the ironies of instructional design: The better the course goes, the less chance there is that anyone will appreciate the effort that went into it.

Designers who use the design and lesson plan approach presented in this book have the opportunity to combine a number of ISD skills and, consequently, to construct almost any training project that makes its way to their door. Most designers incorporate elements of a design plan or a lesson plan in their work although they may never have known what each separate element is called or even its full value. For example, a designer may have incorporated a course rationale into a verbal presentation to a client without understanding why it made a difference to the course, or a designer may have written facilitator prerequisites without studying why they matter in the project. In the case of lesson plans, many designers use some type of format, but may have never realized that there was a sequence that supports the way a participant learns and retains information. Without a complete understanding of the elements of the design and lesson plans, designers may not take the necessary steps consistently and may not follow through with them in a way that will benefit the learners.

Designers' jobs are easier when they see ISD as a process and apply names to the different elements. Their good instincts about how best to design a project, combined with a systems approach to training and education, provide a solid foundation for design.

Following is an overview of this book's systems approach to developing training. ISD is represented by a number of well-thought-out models, but designers most commonly use the ADDIE model. Designers should work toward developing their own ISD model based on their experience and support systems, including this book. Most designers end up doing that anyway, although most are unaware of what they have created.

Reviewing the ADDIE Model

A summary of each of the five elements in the ADDIE model of ISD follows.

Analysis

During the analysis phase of ISD, a designer needs to make sure that every atom of data is collected. Designers need to be data magnets and attract everything of value into the design process. They must

- ask every question and not move on without an answer
- fill boxes full of results from web searches or other data if necessary
- conduct focus groups or undertake other data-gathering methods as necessary.

When they have gathered all the data, designers need to ask four questions:

1. *How will learners be different after the training?* Will they have a new skill, knowledge, or ability, such as enhanced language capabilities or a better way to

process anger in the workplace? Designers should always determine the objectives.

2. *How will learners meet the objectives?* Have the distribution and instructional methods been selected? The choices are endless, but designers must decide methods early in the process to eliminate wasted time and energy later.

3. *How will designers know when the learners have met the objectives?* Have designers decided which of the evaluation methods are appropriate for their objectives and methods? Designers should prepare evaluations at the same time that they write the objectives.

4. *How does the sponsor of the training define success?* If the sponsor's expectations are unknown, there is little chance of ever making him or her happy. It is almost impossible to hit a moving target. Designers have to ask until they get an answer.

Design

Design is the unique element of ISD, with no professional equivalent in other fields. It is here that the project gets a designer's touch. Designers prepare the objectives and evaluation tasks—writing, rewriting, and writing again until they work. They choose the distribution and instructional methods and prepare drafts of materials and media. During design, the data gathered in analysis evolves into the clarity and purpose that a project needs to be successful. A design plan becomes the blueprint for the rest of a project.

Development

Development is pasting the project together. Sometimes designers do it all and develop their own materials and media. Other times they are responsible for managing the process. It can be challenging to work with computer programmers, graphic artists, compositors, video producers, and printers, but it is also satisfying to see ideas become great materials, ready for final production after pilot testing.

Pilot testing ensures that a project is ready for the big time before it moves to implementation. Actors rehearse their lines before a play opens, and musicians practice for hours to perfect a melody before an audience hears a note. In similar fashion, designers use pilot tests to give training an opportunity to muff its lines or hit a wrong note before learners have an opportunity to take a course.

Designers shouldn't get discouraged if they end up doing the design and development work without any help. Multimedia CDs, four-color manuals, and videos with high production values are the exception to the rule for training design. Most organizations can't afford to implement every project on the web or have materials that have the appearance of a coffee table book. The resources and funding for design work are still largely limited.

Implementation

Implementation usually finds designers in front of the learners or in back of them. Designers may be facilitating, evaluating, or both. Until people outside of the process of ISD acquire an appreciation for all the work that goes into it, they are not likely to be aware of any ISD element but implementation. However, designers know that implementation is the ISD equivalent of hanging a newly completed painting. The work is now ready for appreciation.

Designers make sure that the evaluation plan is in effect and that all of the information from the evaluation process is gathered. The facilitator may make necessary changes in the training on the fly during implementation, or the designer will make them later as the dust settles.

Evaluation

Evaluation, the fifth element in the ADDIE model, is always looking over a designer's shoulders. Just as three-year-old children believe that Santa knows if they have been good or bad, evaluation always knows whether training has met the mark. Santa and evaluation share the same quality of vigilance. The difference between good training and bad training is listening to what evaluation has to say. This is hard to do if a designer does not allow evaluation to be a major component of the design process.

Kirkpatrick (1998) has given designers a brilliant framework for evaluation: four different boxes into which most evaluation needs fit. A designer may want to use two, three, or all of these levels of evaluation, depending on the needs.

Level 1 evaluations are based on learners' reactions to training. Did they like it? Did they find it worth their investment of time? Did the distribution and instructional methods find favor with the learners? Were the bagels fresh and the coffee hot? These are all reactions to the training, every single moment of it.

Level 2 evaluations are the same as the evaluations written for objectives. Designers are measuring each learner's ability to meet an objective. Designers must always be sure that the learner is meeting objectives.

Level 3 evaluations are the way to determine if the training made any difference in a learner's ability to meet the objectives. It is not unusual for evaluations to be performed 3, 6, or even 12 months after the training. This information allows a designer to compare results and determine the staying power of the training.

Level 4 evaluations measure the business-level impact or return-on-investment (ROI) of a project. Although usually best left to the accountants because of the financial nature of the process, level 4 evaluation has a place in most projects, and designers should not ignore the long-term value that it brings. Large corporations can calculate business impact in the millions of dollars; a community group can figure the bottom-line impact by the number of new adult readers who can perform a valuable skill. Either way, designers' work has value, and they should think about the effect the training may have on the learner or sponsor.

Accumulation of Advantages

The introduction to this book mentioned the term *accumulation of advantages*. It is the process of performing a number of separate design skills that meld together to become a finished design project. All of the ADDIE elements need to be present for an accumulation of advantages to exist. Doing less than five phases, such as eliminating analysis and evaluation, offers little hope for a successful training project. Accumulate all of the advantages offered by using ISD and reap the benefits of well-conceived and delivered training.

Rechecking Your Skills

Now that you have completed all of the chapters, you can evaluate how your ending skills compare with those when you began this book. This is a pre/post evaluation of your progress. Look again at the list in table 1.1 and answer the questions "yes" or "no." When you are done, compare your answers to the skills inventory you completed when you first read the Introduction. How did you do? If you are still uncertain about any of these instructional design elements, review the chapter associated with the skill.

The Power of ISD

The real power of ISD lies in its ability to provide a foundation for the instructional design process. The work that builds from this foundation can have numerous variations to fit designers' changing needs. The system itself is endlessly evolving within the mind and imagination of each individual designer. This process is only as rigid as a designer wants it to be.

Feel free to play a dominant role in the evolution of the ISD process by revising the ideas in this book to fit your particular needs. With the new skills now in your inventory, you should be ready to meet any design challenge.

Glossary of
ISD Terms

Accumulation of advantages

A chess term referring to the idea that no chess game can be won in one move, but must be the result of many successful moves. In ISD it means that all elements of ISD must be followed in order to ensure successful course development.

ADDIE

The generic ISD model that contains the elements of analysis, design, development, implementation, and evaluation.

Analysis

The first step in the ADDIE model and the starting point for the instructional design process. This is when all design questions are identified and divided into discreet elements for review. Instructional design issues are then addressed as necessary in preparation for the design element of the ADDIE model.

Application feedback—level 1

The first of the interactive elements in the nine events of instruction and the place in a lesson plan where learners are first given an opportunity to practice the content and receive any necessary feedback. The learner and facilitator are equally involved in this process.

Application feedback—level 2

The second of the interactive elements in the nine events of instruction and the second place in a lesson plan where learners are provided an opportunity to practice the content and receive any necessary feedback. The learner is given more control of the application process than in application feedback level 1.

Application feedback—level 3

The third of the interactive elements in the nine events of instruction and the third opportunity for learners to practice the content and receive any necessary feedback prior to a formal evaluation. The learner generally has most of the control of the application process and only receives supportive feedback as necessary.

Asynchronous

When online learning does not take place synchronously and learners are not necessarily in a course participating at the same time.

Audience

The element of an objective that describes in detail the intended learner.

Behavior

The element of an objective that details the expected observable and measurable actions of a learner to reach mastery.

Behavioral objective

(See *objective.*)

Behaviorism

A learning theory that represents the idea that behaviors are often acquired and improved through the use of structured learning opportunities using objectives and observable, measurable evaluations.

Bloom's taxonomy

A hierarchical approach to clustering learning behaviors by relative difficulty.

Chat room

The area within an online course that is used for synchronous activities.

Closure

The last of the nine events of instruction and the element that provides a capsule review of content while also providing a cognitive link for any instruction that may follow.

Cognitive domain

An objective domain that relates to objectives primarily mastered by a student speaking or writing.

Cohort

A group of learners taking one or more courses together as a single group.

Condition

The element of an objective that describes the conditions of learning given in an objective to support mastery. Usually starts with wording such as "given...."

Constructivist

The theory that views learning as a process of facilitation of learners as opposed to a more formal instructor-centered approach.

Content

The fourth element of the nine events of instruction that contains most of the original material or content within a lesson.

Content mastery continuum

The way to measure learner mastery on a continuum from novice to expert.

Course

A unit of learning consisting of one or more modules.

Course description

The design plan element that contains all of the specific requirements for a course to be implemented, such as delivery time, materials, room setup, audio and video requirements, etc.

Criticality

The process of rating content for determining inclusion in a course.

Degree

The element of an objective that specifies the specific evaluative criteria for mastery of an objective.

Degree of difficulty

The relative level of mastery as related to the mastery continuum.

Deliverables

The tangible items required during the design process.

Delivery system

The instructional system used to deliver learning to a student.

Demographics

In analysis, the census-like data that is related to variables like age, gender, education level, and occupation.

Design

The element in the ADDIE model that relates to the design function.

Design plan

The working document developed and used by instructional designers in ISD.

Development

The element in the ADDIE model that relates to the development function.

Direction

The second element in the nine events of instruction; it contains the behavioral objectives for a learning unit.

Discussion board

The element of online learning where learners post assignments and messages to an assigned area within a course.

Distance learning

A generic term for any learning that takes place when the teacher and student are not located in the same place.

Draft objective

A non-formal objective used prior to writing a formal four-part objective.

Enabling objective

Those objectives that support a terminal objective.

Evaluation

Fifth element in the ADDIE ISD model; it encompasses all evaluative methods associated with the instructional design process.

Evaluation strategy

The design philosophy and intent for any evaluation process or product.

Evaluation tasks

The evaluation element in performance agreement.

Facilitator prerequisites

The skills needed to facilitate a course, usually an element in a design plan.

Focus group

A group that represents or includes learners for a specific course or program who are asked specific questions related to the intended content or course.

Formative evaluation

The evaluation of a segment of a unit of learning.

Gagne's Nine Events of Instruction

The sequential elements of learning used in some fashion in most lesson plans.

Gaining attention

The first element in the nine events of instruction; used to gain a learner's attention before new material is presented.

Goals

Generalized and usually non-specific objectives.

Implementation

The element of the ADDIE model that represents the time when a course is actually implemented to the intended population.

Instructional method

The way in which a specific segment of a unit of instruction is presented; examples are lecture, role play, and case study.

Instructional system

Any group of diverse elements that work together to make the development of curriculum more efficient based on systems theory.

Interpersonal domain

An objective domain that relates to objectives primarily mastered by a student communicating in some way with another person or group.

ISD

Instructional systems development; a systems approach to developing curriculum.

ISD model

Any of a number of theoretical models that represent the way instructional design is structured.

Kirkpatrick's Four Levels of Evaluation

A model for evaluation that includes four separate areas of concentration, including reaction, learning, behavior, and return on investment.

Learner prerequisites

Requirements necessary for a learner to participate in a course.

Learning

The act of storing information and data in long-term memory.

Learning management system

Any of a variety of online interfaces between learners, facilitators, and the content of a course.

Lesson

A unit of instruction.

Lesson plan

A detailed guide to the implementation of a lesson usually written in the nine-events format.

Level 1 evaluation

A level 1 evaluation measures the reaction of the learner to the experience; sometimes called smile sheets.

Level 2 evaluation

A level 2 evaluation measures learning and determines if mastery is achieved at the end of a course.

Level 3 evaluation

A level 3 evaluation measures learner behavior after a course and determines if the learning influenced behavior in any way.

Level 4 evaluation

A level 4 evaluation measures return-on-investment (ROI).

LMS

(See *learning management system*.)

Mandated training

Any training that is required by legislation, regulation, or policy.

Mastery

The ability of a learner to complete a behavioral objective to the required specifications.

Mastery tipping point

The point in a lesson or group of lessons that the objective domain and evaluation domain "tip" or change from one to another.

Module

A single learning unit.

Objective

The formal definition of the audience, behavior, condition, and degree required for mastery of knowledge, skill, or other definable behavior.

Objective domain

A classification of objectives referring to the predominant learning focus of either cognitive, psychomotor, interpersonal, or affective.

Online learning

Lessons requiring learners to use Internet or intranet technology to access and participate.

Performance agreement

The relationship between an objective and an evaluation task; performance agreement requires objective and evaluation task to match in behavior, condition, and degree.

Pilot testing

The presentation of a course for the purpose of review and revision prior to general implementation.

Population

A group of learners, generally for a specific course or program.

Population analysis

The process of gathering and analyzing data related to a specific population during an instructional design project.

Posting

The act of a learner placing data in a course for review in online learning.

Prerequisites

The knowledge, skills, or abilities required before participating in or facilitating a unit of instruction.

Pro bono

A professional service performed without compensation.

Process objective

A less formal objective used in the early stages of the design process.

Project

The design and development of learning units using the ISD process.

Psychomotor domain

An objective domain that relates to objectives primarily mastered by a student completing a task requiring physical activity.

QRDP

Quality rating for design plans; a quality control instrument.

QRLP

Quality rating for lesson plans; a quality control instrument.

QRO

Quality rating for objectives; a quality control instrument.

Rationale

In a design plan, the element that serves as the overview of a project.

Reaction

The level of evaluation that represents a learner's immediate feelings related to an instructional event.

Recall

The third of the nine events of instruction; requires the recall of previous learned information for the purpose of building a foundation for new content.

Return-on-investment (ROI)

One of the four levels of evaluation; it assesses the monetary or other benefit derived from a project over and above the cost.

ROI

(See *return-on-investment.*)

Role conflict

When a designer tries to play more than one key role in a design project, like designer and subject matter expert

SME

(See *subject matter expert.*)

Social networking

Any of a variety of digital media that allows interpersonal communications in either synchronous or asynchronous environments.

Subject matter expert

Any of a variety of professionals who provide subject-specific data and support to the instructional design process.

Survey

An analysis and evaluation tool used to gather data that is usually a formal written document that may be either online or printed for distribution.

Synchronous

When learners participating in online learning are in communications at the same time without any delay, such as in a chat room.

Target population

The learners for any instructional design project.

Task analysis

The process of gathering data related to mastery of a specific task or skill for the purposes of designing a unit of instruction.

Terminal objective

The objective that reflects the end or terminal behavior for a lesson, course, or program.

Train-the-trainer course

A course that instructs facilitators in the implementation of a specific unit of learning.

◆ References

Bassi, L.J., and M.E. Van Buren. (1999). *ASTD State of the Industry Report*. Alexandria, VA: ASTD Press.

Gagne, R.M., L.J. Briggs, and W.W. Wager. (1988). *Principles of Instructional Design* (3rd edition). New York: Holt, Rinehart & Winston.

Johnson, J., J. Robinson, and S. Welch. (2004). *Pocket Guide to College Credits and Degrees: Valuable Information for Adult Learners*. Washington, D.C.: American Council on Education.

Kirkpatrick, D. (1998). *Evaluating Training Programs: The Four Levels* (2nd edition). San Francisco: Berrett-Koehler.

Moore, Gordon E. (1965). "Cramming More Components onto Integrated Circuits." *Electronics Magazine* 39:4.

Romiszowski, A.J. (1981). "The How and Why of Performance Objectives." In *Designing Instructional Systems*. New York and London: Kogan Page Limited/Nichols Publishing Company.

Tapscott, Don. (2009). *Growing Up Digital: How the Net Generation Is Changing Your World*. New York: McGraw-Hill.

◆ About the Author

Chuck Hodell is the associate director of the graduate program in ISD at the University of Maryland Baltimore County in Catonsville, Maryland as well as an affiliate assistant professor within the university's language, literacy, and culture doctoral program. He is past deputy provost of the National Labor College in Silver Spring, Maryland. He holds a doctoral degree in language, literacy, and culture and a master's degree in instructional systems development from UMBC. His undergraduate degree is from Antioch University. Chuck has written extensively for ASTD, including participation in the ASTD Learning System program, authoring an anthology of ISD, and authoring several of the popular *Infoline* collection. He is active in his community and serves as the RACES officer in the Department of Emergency Management for Queen Anne's County, Maryland. Chuck's vocational experience includes stints as a musician, a police officer, and he has worked on training and education projects around the world. He resides with his family on Kent Island in Maryland's Eastern Shore. Chuck can be contacted by email at hodell@me.com.

◆ Index